Recollective Resolve

Recollective Resolve

*A Phenomenological
Understanding
of Time and Myth*

Sanford Krolick

 Mercer
University Press

ISBN 0-86554-248-1

The paper used in this publication meets
the minimum requirements of American National Standard
for Information Sciences—Permanence of Paper
for Printed Library Materials, ANSI Z39.48–1984.

Library of Congress Cataloging-in-Publication Data
Krolick, Sanford. 1953–
    Recollective resolve.

    Bibliography: p. 115
    Includes index.
    1. Existential phenomenology. 2. Myth. 3. Time.
I. Title.
B818.5.K76 1987   291.1'3'01   87-1581
ISBN 0-86554-248-1 (alk. paper)

Contents

For my loving wife
Lynda Anne Krolick

Acknowledgments

Many people have given their time, concern, and support to this project. I extend my sincere appreciation to those caring folks and friends. My chief mentor, Dan Via, and his wife, Margaret, surely top the list. Not only have they offered me intellectual stimulation and their unqualified support over the past ten years, but their personal friendship has meant more to me than I can ever express. Although we are now separated by an entire country, our friendship continues to be a rich, enduring source of strength.

I am grateful for the enthusiasm and support of other mentors as well. I thank Bob Scharlemann for his memorable insistence on intellectual honesty and rigor during the past three years. I also thank Ben Ray and David Sapir for their open-mindedness as kind readers of this book in its earliest form. I have benefited from the help of Mircea Eliade, Julian Hartt, Kyle McCarter, Paul Ricoeur, Nathan Scott, and Jacques Taminiaux. To my first professional models, Marvin Bram and Eugene Bär, I am eternally grateful for giving me a thirst for knowledge and a passion for teaching.

Special thanks go to my colleagues and friends Betty Cannon, Pete Hartley, Graham Hereford, and Gloria Kindsvater, all of whom supported and encouraged me while I was teaching and writing during the past four years at the Colorado School of Mines.

Finally, I thank my wife, Lynda, most of all. The innumerable late nights and long weekends that I spent writing, rewriting, and revising must have taken their toll on her patience; but if they have, I really can't tell. She is still as understanding and as caring as the day we met.

Introduction:
What is the Phenomenology of Religion?

In a 1970 article entitled "Is Phenomenology a Method for the Study of Religion?" Hans Penner wrote: "The task of writing a phenomenology of religion remains to be done."[1] It is ironic that such a statement should be made almost ten years after publication of the paperback editions of the two most significant works in the large body of literature that claims to represent the phenomenology of religion. Precisely because of its irony, however, this remark voices my underlying concern—that the phenomenology of religion has existed in a state of crisis since its inception. In the present book I have sought to articulate the nature of the crisis as well as to suggest a more rigorous foundation for future research in the field.

That such a crisis exists will be evident to anyone who attempts to define the phenomenology of religion. Definition is a frustrating exercise because the several notions regarding phenomenology's meaning are confused and contradictory, as are opinions regarding its proper application in the study of religion. Very often "phenomenology" is used to denote reflection that lacks methodological rigor; in other instances, it seems to mean ordinary description.

Again, there is considerable irony in the coexistence of such views. On the one hand, phenomenology as conceived and practiced among its founders in Europe aspires to, if it does not demonstrate, the exercise of remarkable methodological rigor. Furthermore, pure phenomenology cannot legitimately be understood as a positivistic

---

[1]Hans Penner, "Is Phenomenology a Method for the Study of Religion?" *Bucknell Review* 18:3 (Winter 1970): 50.

method for describing and correlating mundane facts. That is not to deny, of course, that phenomenology as currently employed by historians of religion does appear as a not-so-rigorous method for classifying various groups of religious objects and activities by means of a descriptive typology based upon comparative procedures. Indeed such an understanding is quite evident in the work of two very prominent practitioners in the history of religions today, Mircea Eliade (*Patterns in Comparative Religion*) and Gerhardus van Der Leeuw (*Religion in Essence and Manifestation*).

Such a descriptive-typological approach to the phenomenology of religion is unquestionably at least somewhat based on the comparative history of religion first elaborated by the Dutch scholar P. D. Chantepie de la Saussaye in his *Lehrbuch der Religionsgeschichte*. Chantepie's work opens with a phenomenological section that seeks to order "the main groups of religious phenomena without explaining them by doctrinaire reduction, in such a way that the most important aspects and viewpoints emerged from the material itself."[2] Unfortunately, however, a view such as Chantepie's tends to overlook the fact that, when one's consciously doctrinaire biases are bracketed, there still remains the greatest and most pervasive bias of all—the hidden preconceptions of a naively positivistic and empirical point of view, Husserl's "natural attitude."

Nevertheless, while Chantepie's work exerted significant influence on subsequent movements in the history or phenomenology of religion, it should also be acknowledged that the burgeoning of such a " 'science' of Comparative Religions cannot be separated from nineteenth-century scientific thought in general."[3] Indeed, in the early part of the twentieth century, when "Louis Jordan defended the legitimacy of Comparative Religions to claim for itself the title of a 'science,' he pointed to analogues in the field of Comparative Anatomy and Comparative Philology."[4] Goethe, one of the first to coin the term

---

[2]Herbert Spiegelberg, *The Phenomenological Movement* (The Hague: Martinus Nijhoff, 1978) 10 (italics added).

[3]Jonathan Z. Smith, "Adde Parvum Parvo Magnus Acervus," in *Map Is Not Territory* (Leiden: Brill, 1978) 254.

[4]Ibid.

"morphology" in this respect, understood with the anatomists that their discipline was "scientific" by virtue of the method of comparison itself.[5]

Reflecting on the task of the comparative approach to the history or phenomenology of religions, Van der Leeuw suggests that the goal is to develop a typology of the religious phenomena themselves. "The 'Type' in itself has no reality; nor is it a photograph of reality. Like structure, it is timeless and need not actually occur in history."[6] Here Van der Leeuw sounds very much like Goethe, whose "scheme was a typological series that was fundamentally ahistorical while emphasizing the most complex dialectic between the universal and the particular, between ideal and experience."[7] The type was an Ur-phenomenon, "beyond the vicissitudes of time."[8]

Noting that the comparative typological method pervaded research in the history of religions, Jonathan Z. Smith observed that Goethe's discussion of morphology seems to underlie Eliade's own use of such terms.

> When I read in Eliade his numerous and central references to *un système cohérent* behind the various manifestations and hierophanies . . . , when he insists that this *système* nowhere exists but that the archetypes pre-exist any particular manifestation, that the *systèmes* "manifest more clearly, more fully and with greater coherence what the hierophanies manifest in an individual, local and successive fashion"—I am reminded of Goethe's own morphological enterprise.[9]

In any event, it quickly becomes evident that Chantepie's original call for fidelity to facts—the material itself—fell on deaf ears. Instead, the new descriptive phenomenology of religions fostered an idealist position in which the local facts of empirical research pale before clearer and more coherent archetypes or typological systems.

---

[5]Ibid., 255.

[6]Gerhardus Van der Leeuw, *Religion in Essence and Manifestation* (New York: Harper and Row, 1963) 673.

[7]Smith, "Adde Parvum," 256-57.

[8]Ibid., 257, 255.

[9]Ibid., 258 (italics added).

Finally, then, for both Eliade and Van der Leeuw as for the earlier comparativists, the Type—as a universal template of reality—is the explanatory device par excellence. On the one hand, it is an ideal form, distilled from a comparison of all the plurality of actual facts encountered in the world. On the other hand, it is a timeless archetype antedating any and all of those particular instances of its historical occurrence. Either way, it is a purely formal structure, an ideal logical construct that gives to all actual events their universal significance and comprehensibility within a lawful and scientific *système*.

Now, such a typology or taxonomy of the manifestations of the sacred is certainly a legitimate enterprise for the science or comparative history of religions. Yet we are warned that we must never confuse a "mere typology" of religion with a genuine phenomenology, one that attempts to articulate the "essential structure" of religious acts and events.[10] If so, however, what is the difference between the essential structures and relations presumably disclosed by a genuinely philosophical phenomenology of religious experience and the ideal types constructed by a descriptive morphology of the sacred? Why does such a typologizing of religious facts and institutions not constitute a phenomenology of religion in the truly philosophical sense of that word?

Describing the tasks of the historian of religion, Eliade maintains that the historian

> uses an *empirical method* of approach. He is concerned with *religio-historical facts* which he seeks to understand and to make intelligible to others. ... Of course, the historian of religions is also led to *systematize* the results of his findings and to *reflect on the structure of the religious phenomena.* But [in this respect] he completes his historical work as phenomenologist or philosopher of religion.[11]

With these brief remarks Eliade allows us to see exactly where the heart of the crisis in phenomenology of religion lies, for the passage raises several critical questions. How does the historian systematize his findings? How does he make judgments concerning the structure

---

[10]Spiegelberg, *The Phenomenological Movement,* 11.

[11]Mircea Eliade, *History of Religions: Essays in Methodology* (Chicago: University of Chicago Press, 1973) 88.

of religious phenomena? Indeed, how does the historian so easily assume the role of philosopher of religion?

First, the historian of religion develops his generalizations by comparing diverse historical "facts" that have been culled from an empirical method of research. He then orders these different facts according to some classificatory principle that has been inductively derived from the facts themselves. While this may be a legitimate task for the historian, however, it is certainly not the procedure of a phenomenologist. Indeed, as Husserl noted time and again, phenomenology is not a matter-of-fact science; "it does not deal with actual instances, in the sense that it just records and explores these and then makes inductive generalizations from them."[12]

Actually, the phenomenologist's task, qua philosopher, is not to construct logical connections between discrete historical facts but to disclose the intentional relations that are given with the very structure of experience and that *precede* any viewing of such phenomena as independently existing facts. Because scientific historians begin with an empirical method that positivistically defines facts as "isolated, accidental and nonintentional entities," they are already at a second remove from the phenomena that they seek to describe and are therefore unable to discover any underlying *intentional* relations between the different entities. Indeed, they have precluded the possibility of such "intentionality-laden conjunctions" from the very outset by adopting an empirical-positivistic definition of a historical fact.[13] For this reason, historians are restricted simply to drawing (that is, constructing) logical or causal connections between their diverse religiohistorical facts.

The religious historian's view of phenomenology, as an empirical and comparative method of constructing typologies of religiohistorical facts has a problem, in short: the structural relations that this approach reveals refer only to conditions obtaining at a purely naturalistic or *ontic* level—that is, simply to connections between inner-worldly objects. The *ideal types* elaborated by this method are

---

[12]Gilbert Ryle, "Heidegger's *Sein und Zeit*," in M. Murray, ed., *Heidegger and Modern Philosophy* (New Haven: Yale University Press, 1978) 54.

[13]See Calvin Schrag, *Radical Reflection and the Origin of the Human Sciences* (Bloomington: Indiana University Press, 1980) 86-87.

no more than generalizations from observation that have been synthesized and constructed according to some ordering principle discovered by means of the comparison itself. Such an approach succeeds in offering no more than a way of rationalizing similarities that obtain between diverse religious objects and appearances. It does not really illuminate the essential structures that are the very condition for the possibility of the religious mode of being. Heidegger confirms this point himself in *Being and Time.*

> We shall not get a genuine knowledge of *essences* simply by the syncretistic activity of universal comparison and classification. Subjecting the manifold to tabulation does not ensure any actual understanding of what lies before us as thus set in order. If *an ordering principle* is genuine, it has its own content as a thing [*Sachgehalt*], which is never to be found by means of such ordering, but *is already presupposed in it.* So if one is to put various pictures of the world in order, one must have an explicit idea of the world as such. And if the 'world' itself is something constitutive for Dasein, one must have an insight into Dasein's basic structures in order to treat the world-phenomenon conceptually.[14]

Hence an explicit ontology is required despite the positivistic eschewal of ontology. Indeed, only a fundamental analysis of human being can provide the necessary foundation for a genuine phenomenology of religion. Such an analysis is essential if phenomenology is to become more than, other than, a history of religions.

What, then, is the positive task of a genuine phenomenology of religion? First, pure phenomenology is expressly concerned to articulate the *intentional* structure of human existence. The phenomenologist wants to describe the unified totality of being-in-the-world on the far side of any separation of experiencing subject from the objects of experience. He wants to demonstrate those forces that bind the subject to his world and thus constitute the fundamental *structure* of a meaningful existence. In so doing he will be making an ontological description as opposed to an empirical description of objective historical or natural events.

Actually, a phenomenologist may offer ontological descriptions of various modalities of human being in the world. Accordingly, a

---

[14]Martin Heidegger, *Being and Time,* trans. E. Robinson and J. Macquarrie (New York: Harper, 1962) 77.

phenomenology of religion will be concerned with disclosing the structures of religious being by means of an analysis of religious phenomena. It has been suggested, for example, if a genuine phenomenology of religion is to become an actuality, it will, among other things, have to include an analysis of myth and ritual as religious phenomena. "What a phenomenology of religion would have to show is that myths as expressions already have signification. It would then have to be determined what this signification is and how it is given by means of an *intentional analysis.*"[15] An intentional analysis, however, seeks to disclose the correlativity of subject and world and the forces that bind them together. In other words, it describes the fundamental structure of a particular mode of being in the world.

There is thus a need for an analysis of the structure of mythic existence, but the prerequisite for an intentional analysis of any mode of being, mythic or otherwise, is insight into man's basic structures. The phenomenologist of religion will have to begin his work with some analytic of human existence, which will afford the researcher a set of ontological categories to use in approaching the religious phenomena—in this case various myths and rituals. With these categories in hand, the phenomenologist should then be able to show *how* the religious phenomena under investigation do in fact disclose the fundamental structures of human existence, and in this way he will be able to articulate the unique *meaning* of *mythic being* in the world. Among its other tasks, then, a phenomenology of religion must consider myth as a possible mode of being in the world and demonstrate how "man's mythical mode of being is related to the basic mode of man's being."[16]

Finally, a genuine phenomenology of religion, one constituted by this initial ontological motivation, does not work on the empirical level as a comparative science of facts (as does anthropology, ethnology, or the history of religions, for example) but rather seeks to disclose those underlying "intentional" relations in view of which religious or mythic existence occurs as one *possible* mode of man's being in the world.

---

[15]Penner, "Is Phenomenology . . . ?"52, 53.

[16]Joseph Kockelmanns, "On Myth and Its Relationship to Hermeneutics," *Cultural Hermeneutics* 1 (1973): 68.

Part I

Philosophical Anthropology

*Before we can view myth as a unique possibility for human exis-
tence, we must make a preliminary investigation into the problematic of philosophical anthropology, or the philosophical study of
man. In this context, we need to develop a concept of human existence (of man's nature and possibilities) that will allow even the
mythic dimension to become recognizable in its most fundamental
terms.*

*In order to display the ground or nature of mythic existence, how-
ever, we must discover an appropriate methodological orientation.
Our method must be sufficiently radical to allow for a concept of
myth noticeably more comprehensive than the narrow anthropological, literary, political, and sociological definitions that have long
bound our thinking. Only in this way will we be able to illuminate
the structure of myth as an existential possibility.*

*At this point it is necessary to make a preliminary decision, a wager,
if you will, regarding the best way of approaching the question of
man's nature and possibilities. My assumption is that it is most fruit-
ful to begin by recapitulating the task of existential phenomenology.
This move is justified by phenomenology's claim to represent just
that* radical *point of departure that I have said is necessary.*

Chapter One

Existential Phenomenology: The Radical Beginning

Following directions from his mentor, Franz Brentano, Husserl sought to demonstrate the essentially intentional character of all acts of consciousness. For Husserl, there is a fundamental correlation of consciousness and its objects. Consciousness is never an empty *cogito,* as it was for Descartes, but is always "consciousness of" something. This is what he meant by the "intentionality of consciousness."

Heidegger's great insight was to see the implications of Husserl's discovery for any future philosophical anthropology. Meditating upon Husserl's analysis of intentionality, and reflecting especially on the "subject" of this correlation, Heidegger was struck by the observation that subjectivity, the *sum* of the *cogito,* is always already presupposed within the intentional act itself. While "Husserl proposes 'to grasp the kind of Being which belongs to *cogitationes*' ... , he does not see that such a grasp presupposes 'the ontological question of the Being of the *sum*', a task he neglects just as Descartes does."[1]

Focusing attention upon the nature (or Being) of the *sum,* Heidegger discovered that the subject originally recognizes itself only

---

[1]Jacques Taminiaux, "Heidegger and Husserl's *Logical Investigations:* In Remembrance of Heidegger's Last Seminar (Zahringen, 1973)," *Research in Phenomenology* 8 (1978): 59.

within the context of a previously constituted environment. That is, the intentional correlation of subject and object always occurs in the midst of an already existing world. For Heidegger, then, the subject is not a lonely cogito, nor even a cogito-cogitatum. Rather, subjectivity is *being-there* in the world, in the midst of objects and instruments that one uses and takes for granted and that give one's world its unique character, meaning and purpose.

Heidegger therefore concludes that subjectivity is not some phantom closed up within a bag of skin. The self is not located *inside* the body, like a ghost in the machine. Rather the subject is always outside itself, already given over to and "absorbed in" (*aufgehen in*) its world.[2] Existence (he calls it *Dasein,* or "being-there") is a standing-out into the world, through which Dasein touches its world and the world touches, or matters to, Dasein. Accordingly, there are innumerable ways in which the subject (Dasein) may be involved with its world. Producing, giving, taking, doing, seeing, attending, hearing, and speaking represent only a few of these modes of engagement. While Heidegger recognizes the true *embodiment* of Dasein's subjectivity in the event of speech, still, in each of these cases, that which is implied but apparently goes unnoticed is the constitutive role of the body itself.

Actually, Heidegger's analyses do in fact point to the centrality of being *situated,* to the centrality of man's embodied dwelling within the world. Because our existence discloses itself in acts of "manipulation and utilization" as well as in attitudes of disinterested looking, taking up a direction, or setting our sights on something,[3] the body must play a crucial role in constituting every form of one's involvement with the world. That is, wherever and whenever I am engaged with my world, such engagement must be rooted in a bodily presence.

Yet even for Husserl it could be argued that "the possibility of intending objects across the flux of sensorial apparitions involves the disclosure of corporeity in the form of a 'position' and 'state' of the subject."[4] Thus there was already precedent within the phenome-

---

[2]Martin Heidegger, *Sein und Zeit* (Tubingen: Max Niemeyer, 1979) 54.

[3]Heidegger, *Being and Time,* 88, 89.

[4]Alphonso Lingis, "Intentionality and Corporeity," in Anna-Teresa Tymieniecka, ed., *Analecta Husserliana* (Dordrecht: Reidel, 1971) 1:79.

nological movement, beginning with Husserl himself, for an analysis of existence in terms of human embodiment. In this respect, the work of Maurice Merleau-Ponty stands without equal in phenomenological literature. As Merleau-Ponty would boldly proclaim in his *Phenomenology of Perception,* "my existence as subjectivity is at one with my existence as body and with the existence of the world."[5]

Disenchanted with the abstract and apparently artificial reconstructions of experience that traditional philosophical anthropology offered, Merleau-Ponty reiterates Husserl's demand for a radical method of pure phenomenological description. With Heidegger, he wants to deconstruct the reified ego that was a consequence of the modern turn toward the subject inaugurated by Descartes and consummated by Kant.[6]

Merleau-Ponty eschews the very project of transcendental reflection, which ultimately seeks to arrive at a concept of transcendental subjectivity. He contends that such a subject is fictitious—a mere construct of the critical method. "In fact," he argues, "the thinking Ego can never abolish its inherence in an individual subject, which knows all things in a particular perspective."[7] In other words, the real subject is an embodied, concretely existing being. In his attempt to overcome the ontological misconceptions of modern philosophical anthropology, Merleau-Ponty thus found it necessary to redescribe even the intentionality of Husserlian transcendental phenomenology.

Merleau-Ponty beings in a traditional Husserlian fashion by calling for a phenomenological reduction. He wants to bracket critical philosophy's concept of "world." He does so in the hope of disclosing what he terms the phenomenal field—the realm of lived experience that is given prior to any objective world. He describes this realm as a "layer of living experience through which other people and things are given to us, the system 'self-others-things' as it comes into being."[8]

---

[5]Maurice Merleau-Ponty, *Phenomenology of Perception,* trans. C. Smith (Garden City NJ: Humanities Press, 1962) 408.

[6]See Otto Muck, *The Transcendental Method* (New York: Herder and Herder, 1968) 56ff.

[7]Merleau-Ponty, *Phenomenology of Perception,* 61.

[8]Ibid, 54, 56, 57.

This field is the ensemble of relations that obtain between a concretely existing subject and the world as lived by that subject. Here we discover, according to Merleau-Ponty, the being-together of self-others-world in a prereflective and living dialectic.

At this juncture Merleau-Ponty goes further even than Heidegger. True, Heidegger moved well beyond Husserl by suggesting that the correlation of consciousness and its object always occurs within an already constituted horizon of meaning or significance, but at this point Merleau-Ponty begins.

Convinced that intentionality has a more fundamental structure, Merleau-Ponty demonstrates an intentionality of act beneath the intentionality of consciousness. This is an "operative" intentionality, disclosed by the "motor power" of corporeity itself. Originally, then, intentionality is not a conscious *je pense* (a cogito) but, rather, a preconscious "I am able," *je peux*.[9] This preconscious or "operative" intentionality of the body is indicated by its motility, power, potentiality (*Seinkönnen*).

The preconscious intentionality or *power* of corporeity is the primordial locus of subjectivity, a subjectivity of the body proper. It gives to all spheres of action and existential involvement their fundamental grounding. Are not all questions of existence—sexuality, marriage, polity, economy, community, exchange, art, religion, and so on—interdependent modalities of our concrete being-in-the-world? Are not these various concerns, in part, different ways of voicing and *co-responding* to our embodied presence in a world, our being-with or being-toward things and other people? Are they not all meaningful gestures that grasp at and respond to our situation, responses that find expression today in the plethora of our discourses in psychoanalysis, sociology, political science, economics, aesthetics, theology, and so forth? Surely, then, as subject, the body is a "meaning-giving existence."[10]

Indeed, in a real sense the perceptivity and motility of the body is already a "nascent logos." Meaning resides in the postures and gestures of the body in its intentional relations to the world in which it dwells. Herein lies the mystery of openness, that bodily presence in

---

[9]Ibid, 137.

[10]Remy Kwant, *The Phenomenological Philosophy of Merleau-Ponty* (Pittsburgh: Duquesne University Press, 1963) 23.

which there occurs "the 'worldling' of an individual world," the ordering of a meaningful cosmos.[11] Merleau-Ponty states the case succinctly when he writes, "I understand the world because there are for me near and far, foregrounds and horizons," a landscape in which things can appear and can acquire significance.[12] Each of my movements is thus the taking up of a position, an acknowledgment of implicitly meaningful relations. "Already the mere presence of a living being transforms the physical world, bringing to view here 'food,' there a 'hiding place,' and giving to 'stimuli' a sense which they have not hitherto possessed."[13]

Thus even (or especially) within the silence of perception and motility, a logos is born. Existence is the silent field of preconceptual significance that offers a potentiality for explicit, and even linguistic, meaning within which man always dwells incarnate. Underlying each spoken or written word, therefore, an attitude is revealed, a particular *existential* sense or direction, a bodily comportment that conditions it.

My body is subject insofar as it opens me onto the world and thereby discloses itself as *mean-ing* and the world as a meaning for me. Accordingly, the initial movement from silence to speech is not from non-meaning to meaning but "rather a movement from the implicit to the explicit, from ambiguity already pregnant with significance to the expressed significance of speech. If meaning is 'born' it is because [the body-subject] is already pregnant with that possibility."[14]

Together, then, Heidegger and Merleau-Ponty moved beyond Husserl in realizing the project of a truly radical philosophical anthropology, on the far side of any distinction between subject and body, self and world. They did so by locating man's intentional life in *Dasein* as being-there in the world, and by further concretizing that place (*da*) through the elaboration of a phenomenological concept of embodied subjectivity.

---

[11]Eugene Kaelin, *Art and Existence* (Lewisburg: Bucknell University Press, 1970) 241.

[12]Merleau-Ponty, *Phenomenology of Perception,* 408.

[13]Ibid., 189.

[14]Don Ihde, "Singing the World: Language and Perception," in G. Gillan, ed., *The Horizons of the Flesh* (Carbondale: Southern Illinois University Press, 1973) 71.

Chapter Two

Embodied Subjectivity

THE GESTURING BODY

Following his analyses of motility and spatial perception, Merleau-Ponty concludes that the body *is* subject insofar as it is a meaning-giving existence. This subjectivity of the body is discernible at its most fundamental level, in the *openness* or intentionality of corporeity.

Our bodies give us the world as a meaningful field, directing us toward things and toward other people. Even in the simple act of pointing, my body is engaged with a world, giving me a position and concrete orientation in the midst of things. In fact, shapes have value, locations meaning, and movements and events significance only because I am already projected upon things through the very flesh, muscles, and image of my body. Physically engaged within a world, my movements, gestures, and even my sight reach out toward inner-worldly objects, qualifying space, illuminating relations, and ultimately giving me a sense of order and orientation.

On the ground of a purely corporeal or "motor intentionality," then, existential meaning and orientation are first established. Yet "meaning" here cannot denote some ideal sense or signification imposed upon things from outside; it is not meant to suggest any abstract representation (*Vorstellung*) of experience. Rather the meaning born of bodily spontaneity and gesture emerges in the event or occurrence of the act itself. My own or another person's movement toward an object is an incipient act of meaning whereby certain relations or events *as* intended come into view and meaningfully enter my world. In fact, "my world" emerges in the first place in this manner.

Gesture, then, discloses the subjectivity of the body, a subjectivity that bears its meaning within itself. Bodily gesture means or intends the world as a correlate of the body-as-subject. Openness is thus the selfhood of the body as meaning.

Heidegger, on the other hand, beginning with a preconception of the subject as Dasein, suggests that this subject embodies itself in the concrete event of language. In speech (*Gerede*) the implicit meaningfulness of man's various projects is articulated. Discourse becomes, for Heidegger, the embodiment of the subject's being-there in the world as meaning.

I will now demonstrate that this subject (Dasein) finds embodiment by virtue of speech much as the body is subject by virtue of its openness to world. That is, I will show that the discourse of the self is functionally the same as the openness of the body. In this equivalence we will discover the unity of body and subject in human existence: in discourse the subject appears *outside itself* as expression, while in openness the body comes *outside itself* as intention. As the body *speaks out* the ground of meaning in gesture, so the subject *embodies* the meaning of being in discourse. Speaking subject and gesturing body are thus reverse sides of a single reality, the meaningful unity of self and body in an articulated whole called being-in-the-world.

THE SPEAKING SUBJECT

Language, and, in its first instance, speech, bestow meaning in the same way that a gesture is meaningful, by embodying an implicit sense within the act. Speech is a real gesture—concrete (oral-aural), positional (disclosing a particular location or perspective), and directed (it intends a meaning and communicates).

With regard to concreteness, a number of authors have observed that the spoken word is an intimate part of present actuality. The very evanescence of speech gives the spoken word a privileged relationship to all concrete presence. Sound and therefore speech "must emanate from a source here and now discernibly active, with the result that involvement with sound is involvement with the present, with here-and-now existence and activity."[1] When we hear a sound in the night we know that something is out there, and when we hear words being spoken, we know that someone is speaking. Some concrete activity is taking place in and through this happening of language in the event of speech.

Still, how does hearing position us vis-à-vis the reality disclosed by sound and by speech in particular? Vision, for example, places us before or in front of a scene or visual field, but what sort of localization do we achieve in the process of aural perception?

Visual perception presents only one side of a given reality at a time and must consequently synthesize the total situation from a variety of perspectives. Sound, on the other hand, discloses a gestalt. It gives me the situation "in the round." At any particular moment, I hear sounds that emanate from behind me as well as those that come from a source in front of me or anywhere else in my vicinity. I am able to (indeed, I must!) hear all of the sounds within my audible field simultaneously.

Here we discover the positional dimension of the spoken word as a gesture. Because sound and hearing disclose the presence of a world that surrounds me and in which I am located, speaking itself may be understood as the explicit taking up of a position whereby my body converts a specific corporeal power into verbal form.

As sound, language is thus concrete and positional. It situates me (as speaker or hearer) within a total context of vital aural relations. Indeed, speech surrounds me, describing the various boundaries of my world, including my relations to a past and a future and to other persons there.

Here, then, we notice a further dimension of the linguistic gesture. When I utter or hear a statement, I find not only that I am located effectively within a world but also that this world is already constituted in part by a linguistic community or tradition. In speaking, I therefore place myself in the midst and at the disposal of a particular

---

[1]Walter J. Ong, S.J., *The Presence of the Word* (Minneapolis: University of Minnesota Press, 1981) 111-12. I do not of course mean to deny that sound also holds a privileged position with respect to temporality. Unlike sight, it has a "before" and an "after." I will discuss this temporalizing capacity of sound further below.

audience or social-linguistic group. In acknowledging this fact we recognize the final dimension of the gestural sense of language—its communicative force.

When I locate myself vis-à-vis the other (or the group), my speech affects the positions and dispositions of my hearers just as their speech affects me. As a gesture, speech is thus an important key to human subjectivity and intersubjectivity—of man's relations to himself and to other persons within the world.

I would contend at this point that speech in its relation to linguistic meaning parallels the physical gesture in its relation to the goal that it intends.[2] If, for example, by using a hammer I embody the goal or intention of building a house, then when I say "the hammer is too heavy," I am not concerned with representing some ideal object or state of affairs but rather am seeking to illuminate the existential significance of a concrete and highly specific situation. In describing the hammer as too heavy, I voice my concern with the task at hand and express my view that the tool is intrinsically inadequate to complete my project fully and successfully. My speech is intended to disclose my concern as well as to inform those with whom I am working that my project may suffer accordingly.

In speaking, as in gesturing, the subject is concerned not with the process of signification but rather with what is meant, pointed out, or intended by the significative act. Furthermore, that which is meant is not some abstract concept or idea but the existential significance of a concrete situation.

Meaning, in other words, always resides in the event of its articulation, whether it be in those inaudible (but never silent) articulations of bodily gesture, in the internally audible articulations of conceptual thought, or in the explicit (oral or written) articulations of verbal behavior. In any event, gestural, conceptual, or verbal images are the *body* of meaning, without which it could not exist. Every thought or idea that reaches even the dimmest light of consciousness has a particular shape, that is, a form that may be articulated in language. Indeed, we might say that thought depends for its very existence upon language and upon the spoken word in particular.

------

[2]Merleau-Ponty, 89.

On the other hand, every word (as meaningful) already rests upon a bodily posture, a *gestural sense* whereby the world is originally taken up understandingly in lived experience. Language is thus *emotive,* speaking *out* the gestural sense that grounds it. Our various bodily perspectives (postures, gestures, movements, and so forth) give us a prepossession of sense, of meaningful presence. Language, in its first and most fundamental movement—as speech—makes explicit that which is already implicit within these bodily gestures. We can begin to see at this point the emergence of a very complex dialectic between bodily gesture, language, and meaning as we enter into the mystery of embodied subjectivity itself.

We recognize, in fact, that the spoken word serves a peculiarly existential function in its potential for disclosing human subjectivity or the intentional structure of being in the world. Because of the complex structure of embodied subjectivity, speech (as gesture) discloses objects and the world as the context of our engagement with them. Furthermore, however, language has the capacity to articulate the essential *care* structure of human being as such. In short, the spoken word is a unique gesture in that it embodies man's being-there-in-the-world in a distinctively human way, permitting the "existential"—intentional and historical—character of man's being to disclose itself.

Even in its apophantic function, where objects originally shine forth, language discloses the situation of the speaker. In noting that the hammer is too heavy, for example, my statement also communicates a dimension of my work world, namely the building of a house. This in turn implies a larger, existential context one—the problem of dwelling as such, a fundamental concern of my "Being-in" in the world.

In other words, that which the linguistic utterance discloses, what it means in its specifically existential function, is neither coincident with the sound-percept nor separate from the word as an external referent. Rather, through the word, in its being heard *as* the speaking *of* language, we hear human being-in-the-world coming to audition in a distinctive way. We grasp the concrete concerns of a conscious subject embodied within the world, in the midst of his daily or even his extraordinary activities. In this way language is truly the *embodiment* of human subjectivity. Speaking, in this case, is a real process of objectification. Bodying forth existence, language exposes the intentional postures of being-*there* in the world.

LANGUAGE AND THE BODY

At this point we need to inquire into the relation between language as the embodiment of the subject and openness as the subjectivity of the body. I do not pretend to grasp the factual origins of language. Rather I want simply to display the fundamental linguisticality of human dwelling.

First, what constitutes the nature of that prethematic, prelinguistic, and even gestural creation of meaning given with corporeity itself? As Heidegger might suggest, such meaning originates in *Geworfenheit* [3]—that is, in man's "being-thrown" or embodied within a specific cultural milieu, finding himself already in the midst of, and belonging to, a unique historical "life world."[4] This life-world is given, moreover, in the "objectifications of life"[5] that constitute any historical tradition and transmit that tradition as a living event in each particular present. Such objectifications include social and political institutions, buildings, customs, beliefs, practices, historical records, works of art, and science and technology. In all the ways in which man's historical existence finds expression, however, the primordial togetherness of man and world is attributable to the speaking of language.

Indeed, language itself allows for the various meaning-structures of man's existence to emerge; it is that horizon within which our concrete historical existence is given to us in all its variety and meaningful objectification. Speaking is, in this view, the fundamental gesture of embodied subjectivity, creating that "open space" or "realm of shared understanding" within which men may exist.[6] In this re-

---

[3]See Heidegger, *Being and Time,* 174ff. and sect. 38.

[4]See, e.g., Edmund Husserl, *The Crisis of European Sciences and Transcendental Phenomenology,* trans. D. Carr (Evanston: Northwestern University Press, 1970) 103-89.

[5]See, e.g., Wilhelm Dilthey, *Pattern and Meaning in History,* ed. H. P. Rickman (New York: Harper and Row, 1962) 123.

[6]R. E. Palmer, *Hermeneutics* (Evanston: Northwestern University Press, 1969) 206.

gard, language provides a framework for understanding new experiences; it allows for their incorporation into a preexisting stock of shared knowledge and values. Language is thus the primary means by which various levels and sedimentations of meaning become transmitted within and throughout a cultural tradition.

Still, this *saying* is not the simple act of man's speaking. Rather it is the originary and productive capacity of a historical tradition itself, a potency that is already present whenever persons take to speaking together. Initially, man's own word is a listening in on the language we speak. Man's role in the speaking of language is primarily a matter of hearing, of being open to that which is said within the tradition and then responding. Man's meaningful placement in the world is thus grounded in his being *as* a *thrown project* or embodied subject, already given over historically to what is opened up by language.

If one retorts that man himself creates and uses language as a tool among other tools, that he alone is responsible for producing language, I would argue that man uses language—that he has the power (*pouvoir*) to speak—only because he first belongs within a historical linguistic tradition. When he is beginning to speak, furthermore, man initially responds with what he has already heard within that tradition.

I thus suggest that the prelinguistic grasping of our existential situation—the implicit meaningfulness of a corporeal existence—is grounded in a total context of meanings given to us in the language we hear and eventually learn to speak. Heidegger's own claim that language is a house in which man dwells suggests that man properly resides first and foremost in language.[7] Like a home, language has a history and a distinctive character. It "calls together the major things associated with human life: security, comfort, family, friends, rest, meals, leisure, as well as the difficulties and problems connected with all of these."[8] Language thus makes a place in which the basic exigencies of the human condition may come into the center of man's concern. In this way, language is called the house of being. It is in language that man truly dwells as man.

---

[7]Martin Heidegger, "The Letter on Humanism," in N. Languilli, ed., *The Existentialist Tradition* (Garden City: Doubleday, 1971) 242ff.

[8]L. M. Vail, *Heidegger and Ontological Difference* (University Park: Pennsylvania State University Press, 1972) 163.

I am not denying here the point I argued above, namely, that meaning (in the sense of a prethematic and corporeal orientation within the world) is an existential possibility given with the very perceptivity and motility of the body itself. While these phenomena, as expressions of man's fundamental openness, pouvoir, or Seinkönnen, however, are necessary conditions for the birth of meaning, they are by no means sufficient conditions for the full articulation of meaning as such.

Indeed, a fully intelligible event of meaning, one both explicit and susceptible to intersubjective agreement, is possible only because man can place his movements (or any other events) within a larger context of relations, a context that extends beyond the immediacy of desire and the givens of his present situation. This capacity for contextualizing experience, however, is available only because man is able to name the various and implicitly meaning-laden events and thereby to coordinate them within greater wholes and relation-schemes that thus constitute the world. Finally, his capacity for naming rests upon his being in the midst of a concrete language, a linguistic tradition with a history and a logic all its own. Man is born into language, and this being-in-language gives him the power of speech and the capacity for articulate meanings much as having a body and limbs gives him the power of gesture and the capacity for a concrete orientation within the world.[9]

Thus while man's openness to world or corporeal intentionality supplies him with a primordial directedness, allowing him the possibility of perspective and a prereflective sense of being in the world, speech "rounds out" and fulfills that original capacity, offering man the articulate meaning of linguistic gestures in a world (not simply an *Umwelt*) that they creatively disclose. In any event, the fact that the openness of the body-subject is essential to the constitution of our basic existential sense and orientation does not deny the creative (indeed, the fundamental) role played by language in making possible such meaningful orientations. On the contrary—only because such openness is characterized by a primordial linguisticality, only because man *is able* to speak a shared language and to under-

---

[9]See Margaret Urban Coyne, "Merleau-Ponty on Language," *International Philosophical Quarterly* 20 (Spring 1980): 313.

stand what is said to him in return—only on this basis are his pre- and nonlinguistic gestures capable of manifesting any meaningful content whatsoever.

In summary, because man is a concretely existing subject, open to the world, he is historical. Because he is historical, man is born into a particular culture. Being cultural, he has and is possessed by language. Only because man stands in the midst of this language are his movements and gestures understood and treated as meaning something. We could say, at this point, that, while the human body is subject because it is open to the world, this openness is itself the font of meaning only because it is essentially a movement toward linguisticality or speech. Embodied subjectivity now means that the body-as-subject is openness to the world that embodies itself in language.

LANGUAGE AND OBJECTIVIZATION

Thus far we have tried to elaborate an understanding of existence in which subjectivity and corporeity find themselves inextricably joined in an originally integrated reality called being-in-the world. So intimate are the connections among all elements of this structural whole (body-subject-world) that any attempt to describe one element without mention of the others would be misleading. There is some indication, however, that the fundamental integrity of this "lived body-world" can become submerged.

Now, before embarking upon our initial consideration of myth and linguisticality, we must first discuss the splitting up of the integrated whole. The epistemological bifurcation of body and subject, together with the correlative disintegration of that fundamental unity called being-in-the-world, I have designated the process of objectivization. Let us consider this process in a general way.

Expressing the intentional postures of a body-subject engaged within its horizon, language invariably speaks out or objectifies experience whereby men and women may communicate and agree upon a world of their common concern. This original and creative self-disclosure or objectification of the lived body-world in speech, however, need not lead to those abstract objectivizations (*Objektivierungen*) that characterize the various realms of modern technical communication. Yet such objectivization does in fact occur.

Heidegger describes this process of a "thematizing" of experience through the establishment of signs that are the result of a purely theoretical intention, developed "in the course of theoretical *speculation*."[10] Various authors have suggested that science gave birth to this speculative process, beginning with the Greeks and culminating in the development of specialized terminologies for all areas of objective inquiry.

As I will argue below, however, wherever words become mere signs, and seeing (*spaeculum*) replaces hearing as the basic mode for understanding or synthesizing experience, the primordial connection between a speaking body and a thinking subject becomes changed into an external, accidental relation. Only then does the reality of human embodiment and the preobjective integrity of our being-in-the-world become submerged. As a consequence of this abstraction, the dichotomy between the subjectivity of the ego cogito and the objectivity of the natural world appears to be an absolutely primordial phenomenon.

In spite of this speculative ideal, however, the life of language remains unchanged. For while speaking itself objectifies experience, it is precisely that—a *Konkretisierung,* or embodiment of meaning, in which the fundamental unity of body-subject and world is revealed rather than covered over. Indeed, the spoken word discloses only a situated subject intimately involved with his intentional surroundings. As with all other bodily gestures, speaking is the event of an embodied subject, a concretely existing individual located within a specific milieu.

Thus despite the advance of objectivizing speculation, man remains oriented concretely in the midst of things: his body, as a thrown-project, gives him varying perspectives within his world. Even his verbal gestures are situated responses, voicing the "intentional arc" that originally unites man with the world of his concern. Precisely by means of its objectifications, then, speech naturally discloses the fundamental coinherence of Dasein's being-there-in-the-world.

Apparently, however, man's original involvement with phenomena, his positional being-there, and its preobjective integrity tends to

----

[10]Heidegger, *Being and Time,* 414, 112.

be submerged. It seems that, while the body gives us an opening on things, it simultaneously permits the impression that a particular thing might be grasped in its entirety. Let us take one example. While "from my window only the tower of the church is visible, . . . this limitation simultaneously holds out the promise that from elsewhere the whole church could be seen."[11] In other words, we assume that we might obtain the view on things, that we might come to *see* things absolutely from an ideal or transcendental perspective, which is no perspective at all. This belief is reinforced in visual experience when, by a process of creative synthesis, we imaginatively project all the sides of an object that are not immediately present to our gaze. Yet in fact, in order

> to view the world around me, I must turn my eyes, taking in one section after another, establishing a sequence. . . . There is no way to view all that is visible around me at once. As Merleau-Ponty has nicely put it in his 'L'Oeil et L'esprit', vision is a dissecting sense. Or, to put it another way, one can say it is sequential. It presents one thing after another. . . . The actuality around me accessible to sight, although it is all simultaneously on hand, can be caught by vision only in a succession of 'fixes'.[12]

Thus we may say that vision performs "no more than a presumptive synthesis. . . . And the positing of the *object* therefore makes us go beyond the limits of our actual [concrete] experience."[13] We thereby synthesize the ideal form of the object as seen by an ideal observer who is nowhere in particular. Through this process of (speculative) idealization or abstraction we fool ourselves into believing that consciousness or thought (that is, pure subjectivity) can extricate itself from any and every finite perspective—indeed, that it can become omniscient and universal. Such belief "suppresses the immediacy of the mind-body relation and constructs an epistemological subject whose sole function is to survey a field of physical objects and relations."[14]

---

[11]Merleau-Ponty, *Phenomenology of Perception,* 90.

[12]Ong, *The Presence,* 129.

[13]Merleau-Ponty, *Phenomenology of Perception,* 70.

[14]John O'Neill, *Perception, Expression, and History* (Evanston: Northwestern University Press, 1970) 14.

Ultimately because of this construction, the preobjective engagement of the lived body-world becomes glossed over and submerged in the interests of an ideal scientific objectivity. Moreover, the abstractions of speculative thinking and conceptualization not only produce the alienation of a newly constructed epistemological subject from the objective world—itself conceived as a fixed and uneventful region of study—but furthermore, and as a corollary, they fracture the life-world itself, creating a series of rifts, insularities, and polarities among a now discontinuous variety of thematic areas for investigation (that is, economics, politics, aesthetics, psychoanalysis, sociology, religion, natural science, and so on). The original integrity of the world-horizon, corresponding to the integrity of the lived-body, is thus glossed over in a plethora of technical distinctions and thematic divisions.

Chapter Three

Language and Myth

My analysis of myth opens with an examination of man's linguistic ability. I consider the specificity of mythic existence in a rather gingerly fashion by grounding the traditional anthropological distinction between preliterate and literate cultures upon a more solidly phenomenological foundation. In conclusion, I raise the question of the identity of mythic subjectivity on the basis of differences that emerge with the shift from oral to written modes of communication.

SPEAKING AND WRITING

At the close of the last chapter, I mentioned the issue of objectivization—the apparent disintegration of that original whole called being-in-the-world. I indicated how this process might relate to the presumptive syntheses of experience that are effected by visual perception and speculative thinking. Now, however, we must address the question "what is the source or mechanism behind this process of objectivization?"

I will contend that the underlying mechanism results from a basic potentiality in the nature of human linguisticality itself. More specifically, the tendency toward objectivization may be understood as a function of changes effected by the shift from a predominantly oral to a basically written technology of communication. Indeed, if embodied subjectivity has come to mean that the body is subject as openness-to-world that embodies itself in language, then a person's experience of being-in-the-world should be responsive to that person's particular mode of linguistic self-disclosure or embodiment. Accordingly, we might suspect that the apparent dissociation of body and subject, together with the abstract thematization of experience, essentially relates to distinctions created by a literate mode of communication versus a nonliterate one.

Numerous researchers have noticed the consequences of shifting from an oral to a written medium. It has been observed, for example, that the spoken word is context dependent. Knowledge gained within an oral communication is immediate, concrete, and specific, tied to the situation of communication between speaker and hearer. As the discursive medium changes from an oral mode to a written one, the message has a tendency to become more generalized and abstract—more objective. No longer bound to the situation of writer or reader, knowledge becomes decontextualized, speculative, and open to greater degrees of analysis and recontextualization.

Bracketing any strictly historical claim at this point, I suggest only that there could be an existential correlation between the conceptual bifurcation of self-world, body-subject unities, and the abstract thematization of experience that appears with the growth of literate culture and more predominantly written forms of communication. Indeed, if human existence is intimately tied up with the way in which it embodies itself in language, then man's experience of being-in-the-world should alter significantly with any change in his linguistic capacities and performances. If so, would not such alteration be especially significant, given that the transformation from an oral to a written medium necessarily entails a correlative shift from basically auditory to predominantly speculative means of synthesizing experience? I will now consider just this possibility.

It has been argued in a variety of contexts that the spoken word (especially in preliterate cultures) has a sacred status, even a mystical quality, contingent upon its felt efficacy or power. This power of the word appears, in turn, to be a function of the unique relationship that sound bears to the vitality of present actuality.[1] Because of sound's unique relationship to active presence, it may be said to have

---

[1]Hans Jonas, *The Phenomenon of Life* (New York: Delta, 1968) 137.

a special force and efficacy, more so than any other sense impression. In fact, "sound signals the present use of power, since sound must be in active production in order to exist at all. . . . Hearing registers force, the dynamic. . . . A primitive hunter [who] . . . hears an elephant trumpeting or merely shuffling his feet . . . had better watch out. Something is going on. Force is operating."[2] Now, if we consider the status of the spoken word within such an aurally dominated world, we might conclude that "cultures which do not reduce words to space [as in written communication] but know them only as oral-aural phenomena, in actuality or in the imagination, naturally regard words as more powerful than do literature cultures. Words *are* powerful."[3] Remnants of this power of the spoken word may be found within our own Western religious heritage, itself rooted in oral tradition. Remember, for example, that Yahweh created the universe through his spoken word. The word of God was powerful; it was creative, sacred power par excellence.

The centrality of the concept of the power of the spoken word within Christianity has prompted one author to suggest a very radical thesis that—given "the conflict between two linguistic modalities, *verbum scriptum* versus *viva vox*"—seeks to "reconnect the belaboured theologoumena of justification by faith and righteousness of God with the oral matrix of the preached gospel."[4] Indeed, Werner Kelber's *The Written and the Oral Gospel* demonstrates that there was a severe rupture in Christian experience when man shifted from an oral to a written medium.

Recalling my discussion of the auditory synthesis, we know that hearing, unlike vision, orients the individual within a gestalt. Sound situates the hearer not simply in front of a screen or visual field but within a total context of aural relations. Moreover, this context is synthesized not sequentially and diachronically, as in visual experience, but instantaneously and synchronically, in a sort of aural harmony, "tunedness," or *Stimmung*—giving one "a sense of unity

---

[2]Ong, *The Presence,* 112.

[3]Ibid.

[4]Werner Kelber, *The Oral and the Written Gospel* (Philadelphia: Fortress, 1983) 141.

working out from the world of sound to all actuality."[5] We now find
that this event is productive of a sacrality or power by virtue of the
vitality of sound and the efficacy of the spoken word itself. In view of
this situation, it may be said that

> the shift in focus from the spoken word and habits of auditory syn-
> thesis to the alphabetized written word and visual synthesis (actual-
> ity is measured by picturability) devitalizes the universe, weakens the
> sense of presence in man's life-world, and in doing so tends to render
> this world profane [that is, lacking an essential unity and vitality], to
> make it an agglomeration of things.[6]

Indeed, I would argue that the effect of writing on language and consequently upon man's overall sense of the power and unity of existence—a unity grounded initially in an auditory synthesis or
harmony—is quite devastating.

Writing has a separating, objectifying effect on language. On the
printed page, words appear removed from actions and events, no
longer directly linked to those realities that they embody. By con-
verting speech into an "object of visual as well as aural inspection,"
writing shifts the primary receptor from ear to eye.[7] And the synthesis achieved by visual inspection is, as we recall, a sequential and
therefore presumptive or constructive synthesis. Only by actually or
imaginatively altering my perspective do I succeed in synthesizing an
object of visual attention or even the entirety of my visual surroundings. Necessarily, however, such a synthesis is abstract and ideal and
presupposes a distanciation of the knowing subject from the actual
world of experience.

We must recall Heidegger's own indictment of the Western meta-
physical tradition at this point insofar as its questioning of being is
"determined by an overemphasis on vision" and static presence. Heidegger himself argued that speculation—making things into objects
by "throwing them up against" a screen for visual inspection—lies at
the root of our modern attempts to objectify or thematize experi-

---

[5]Ong, *The Presence,* 128.

[6]Ibid., 162.

[7]Jack Goody, *The Domestication of the Savage Mind* (New York: Cambridge University Press, 1978) 44.

ence, thereby reducing everything to a mere presence at hand, objective Nature. Preferring the sense of hearing, or "hearkening," to that of seeing, Heidegger pointed out that conscience, our capacity for authentic existence, resides in our listening and attending to the "Call of Being."[8]

In an oral-aural world, then, the synthesis of experience is achieved instantaneously and completely, without any alteration or presumption of point of view or "focus" of attention. Aurally the whole context is given at once, orienting us concretely in the midst of an integrated and powerful world. Indeed, by listening, we can simultaneously recall the past, anticipate a future, and attend to what is present.[9] Hearing surrounds us not only in a spatial sense but also temporally.

I conclude that the grand dichotomy is not between advanced and primitive, "open" and "closed," or domesticated and savage societies. Indeed, there is really no simple dichotomy. Where we discover a radical distinction between self and world, however—wherever the underlying integrity of embodied-subjectivity goes unrecognized—we may also find a predominance of literacy and a shift from oral to written technologies of communication.

It should not be inferred, however, that the basic structure of being-in-the-world is ever overcome. Indeed, could one simply suspend those objectivizing tendencies of visual synthesis that the written word seems to entail, one would uncover the identity in difference, "that subtle knot which makes us man"[10] and always already precedes us in every act of perception, in every gesture and mode of being-there. Thus in spite of the radical objectivization of the existential field, that is to say, regardless of any theoretical bifurcation of self and world and the correlative dividing up of that world into various independent regions, a more fundamental reality remains con-

---

[8]Michael Zimmerman, "Heidegger and Bultmann: Egoism, Sinfulness, and Inauthenticity," *Modern Schoolman* 58 (November 1980): 7. Also see Heidegger, *Being and Time,* 414.

[9]Michael Zimmerman, *Eclipse of the Self* (Athens: Ohio University Press, 1982) 16.

[10]John Donne, "The Extasie," in J. T. Shawcross, ed., *The Complete Poems* (New York: Doubleday, 1967) 132.

cealed, a reality in which one's historical life-world is still close to the natural world-horizon of the prereflective body-as-subject.

As I will argue below, prior to and underlying our technologies of written communication we find the fundamentally integrated experience of the lived body-world as disclosed by the spoken language of myth. I do not suggest that there is no myth after the emergence of writing; rather I mean that, as a way of being, the primordial mythic experience is eclipsed by our various literate and technical thematizations of experience.

I will suggest, in conclusion, that life-world of the myth-making experience is essentially preobjectivized and compact. In this world the intentional relations uniting body-subject and the world-as-lived by the body are not yet lost in abstract categorizations and thematizations. In this world various regions remain relatively intact, experience is a highly compacted form of existential engagement, and voice is therefore the somewhat opaque and highly symbolic language of myth.

THE "WHO" OF DASEIN, THE "WHO" OF MYTH

Another side of this distinction between oral and written technologies of communication has serious implications for the preliminary characterization of mythic existence and the nature of mythic subjectivity. Various authors have suggested that, with the shift to a written medium, there is a correlative growth in individualism. As Walter Ong has written in *The Presence of the Word,*

> with writing, and more intensely with print, the individual first becomes aware of himself as capable of thinking for himself to a degree impossible for relatively overcommunalized tribal man. Without literacy man tends to solve problems in terms of what *people* do or say—in *the tradition* of the tribe [for example, as did our ancestors, as it is told in the myth], without much personal analysis. He lives in what anthropologists call a 'shame' culture, which *institutionalizes public pressures on individuals to ensure conformity* to tribal modes of behavior. With literacy, the individual finds it possible to think through a situation more from within his own mind out of his own personal resources and in terms of an objectively analyzed situation which confronts him. He becomes more original and individual, detribalized.[11]

---

[11]Ong, *The Presence,* 134-35.

While this passage highlights the emergence of individuality vis-à-vis the general topic of personal responsibility, we should consider the issue of creativity in particular. In opposition to creation in an oral medium, where every original is subject to continual recreation and recomposition, and thus where individual achievement seems swallowed up within the larger body of traditional transmission, in literate cultures the composer of a work is recognized as *its author*—that is, as an individual creator.

Individual creativity remains unrecognized in oral cultures, not because it does not exist, but because of the very processes of oral adaptation, processes that both allow for and necessitate creative *re-presentation*. Contrary to being absent in such cultures, creative genius simply becomes lost in the traditional forms of representation and cultural transmission.[12]

There may thus be a form of *anonymity*—or lack of sense of individuality—associated with existence in societies dominated by oral technologies of communication. In these cultures, where everything is passed on by word of mouth, no single individual is ever responsible for a particular statement, position, or point of view. Rather, some ancestor or the tradition has passed on this or that bit of information. A generalized *Other* and never a living member of the tribe is responsible for casting a particular spell, performing a magical cure, or even founding a cultural institution. In preliterate cultures, this anonymous self or generalized Other invariably finds embodiment in the guise of a mythic ancestor or divine personage, *in illo tempore, ab origine.* Each member of the group confers all personal responsibility and creativity (from the simplest ritual act to the creation of a complex public institution) upon that spirit of the group, the divine mythic hero, the creative power par excellence.

We should pause here, however, to consider a more contemporary discussion of anonymity. I refer to Heidegger's analysis of the subjectivity of Dasein in the mode of everydayness. By *Dasein,* Heidegger means the ineluctable character of human existence that I have designated above by the expression "being-in-the-world."

---

[12]Goody, *Domestication,* 27.

More often than not, Dasein is absorbed in and fascinated by its world. We find ourselves alongside things with which we are involved and about which we are concerned. Precisely this character of being absorbed in the world is relevant when we discuss the constitution of subjectivity in terms of its everyday mode of existence.

In each case, whenever Dasein finds itself thrown into a world, that world is always already constituted as a meaningful milieu; the world has been interpreted even before any particular existent finds itself there. In other words, existence is essentially communal. Heidegger uses the expression "being-with" to indicate this potentiality for communion among existing Daseins.[13] One grows up in such communion, disclosing the world as it has been previously constituted and made available by that community. In this manner, Dasein is inexorably dependent upon others. "In everyday life [his] existence seems to be necessarily heteronomous," radically contingent upon how the Others of his community constitute the world.[14]

Herein lies the domination of everyday existence by the anonymous One—*das Man.* So pervasive and tyrannical is this public dominance of *the One* that it "does not tolerate any critique of its authority in any matter, [and] the *personal sense of responsibility is taken away from everybody.* Whatever decision I face, [the One] has long ago prescribed what should be done in such a case." Still, while such domination reduces each person's freedom to choose his own way of interpreting the world, this anonymity also gives the individual a certain sense of security. It allows Dasein to become totally absorbed in the many, to be part of a larger whole, losing itself in pure publicness, forgetting itself, and giving itself over to determination by the group.[15]

While it is important to note how Heidegger's description of everyday existence resembles our account of anonymity in preliterate cultures, mythic anonymity is not to be confused with Heidegger's description. Indeed, as I will show below, the anonymity of mythic Dasein is not, like the everydayness of more highly differentiated Dasein, a flight from authentic being one's self. As Heidegger himself is quick to note, "Everydayness does not coincide with prim-

---

[13]Joseph Kockelmanns, *Martin Heidegger: A First Introduction to His Philosophy* (Pittsburgh: Duquesne University Press, 1965) 54.

[14]Ibid.

[15]Kockelmanns, *Heidegger,* 61.

itiveness, but is rather a mode of Dasein's Being, even when Dasein is active in a highly developed and differentiated culture—and precisely there."[16]

On the other hand, it may be the case that mythic anonymity, where the tribal member identifies himself with the divine ancestor or mythic hero, represents a precritical inability to recognize the "self" independently of the ambiguous power that surrounds it and upon which it depends for its very life. In fact, because of the fundamental integrity of existence in myth-making experience, we should understand mythic anonymity as a condition betraying that sense of the *prepersonal* unity of being-in-the-world, including an undifferentiated sense of being-in-community with that group in which one moves and lives and has one's being. I will suggest, in this regard, that mythic anonymity has a much greater affinity with Merleau-Ponty's concept of *l'On*—the preconscious, prepersonal subjectivity of the body—than with Heidegger's concept of das Man.

Moreover, we should note that, when everyday Dasein loses itself in the anonymity of the public domain, "the One" that answers to the "who" of everyday existence is really a "nobody."[17] That is, everyday Dasein *loses* itself not by identifying itself with some particularized Other but rather by identifying itself with *no one* in particular—simply giving itself up to the "anyone" of pure publicness.

On the other hand, the anonymity associated with mythic existence will be shown to be a mode of being that entails an explicit identification with a particular culture hero or divinity. Accordingly, mythic Dasein does not deny its own existence but rather prethematically understands itself to be taken up into a reality (or Self) greater than itself, that powerful ground upon which its life literally depends.

Thus while literate Dasein's everydayness appears as a flight from authentic selfhood and personal responsibility, a recognition of individual powerlessness, mythic Dasein's engulfment in anonymous, ambiguous power appears to be nothing less than a self-disclosure of that primordial intentionality of embodied subjectivity itself. We will now consider this experience of "power" in the constitution of mythic existence and its self-disclosure in the mythic word.

---

[16]Heidegger, *Being and Time,* 76.

[17]Ibid., 166.

Part II

A Phenomenology
of Mythic Existence

Initially I sought to develop a radical philosophical anthropology as a point of departure for an analytic of mythic existence. Having found such a starting point in the concept of embodied subjectivity, I will now consider the implications of this conception for the philosophical investigation of myth.

In proceeding, I must first make explicit what was only implicit at the close of the last chapter, namely my preliminary conception of mythic existence. To this end, I must distinguish more clearly between Heidegger's concept of everyday existence and mythic being in the world. I will recommend a conception of Dasein as myth maker based upon considerations of human linguisticality and the concrete dichotomy between speaking and writing. Only on this basis is it possible to provide a truly fundamental analysis of mythic existence, addressing those constitutive elements revealed in part one.

Chapter Four

An Approach
to Mythic Existence

In chapter 3 I discussed the "who" of mythic Dasein. I indicated that, while there appear to be similarities between the anonymity of mythic existence and the "lostness" of everyday being-in-the-world, it would be overly hasty simply to assume that these two modalities of existence are identical. I will now conclude the discussion in order to proceed with a more systematic formulation of Dasein as myth maker.

THE FALLING OF EVERYDAY DASEIN AND MYTH

In his analysis of everyday existence, Heidegger insists that "the One" (das Man) is a structural component of being-in-the-world, a concrete expression of our being-with-one-another.

> Dasein, as everyday Being-with-one-another, stands in *subjection* to Others.... What is decisive is just that inconspicuous domination by Others which has already been taken over unawares from Dasein as Being-with. ... 'The Others' ... '*are there*' in everyday Being-with-one-another. The "who" is *not* this one, *not* that one, *not* oneself, *not* some people, and *not* the sum of them all. The 'who' is the neuter [the One] (*das Man*).[1]

---

[1]Heidegger, *Being and Time,* 164.

While "the One" positively determines existence in its everyday being-with-one-another, fundamentally it refers to nothing substantial. Das Man is nothing definite. It is a nobody—"not this one" and "not that one." In other words, "the One" is a way of being through which Dasein escapes itself by letting itself be determined by "no one" or nothing in particular. It takes upon itself the nameless and faceless character of the public domain, denying its selfhood in the process. Dasein flees from itself in everyday existence and thus it is called inauthentic (*uneigentlich*), or not-being-one's-own.

Still, if the mode of being of "the One" is called inauthentic because of not-being-its-Self, then it must presuppose, as the condition for its possibility, authentic being-one's-Self. Indeed, Dasein loses itself in the anonymity of the public domain only by falling away from itself as a self. Says Heidegger, "Dasein has, in the first instance, *fallen away [abgefallen] from itself as an authentic potentiality for Being its Self,* and has fallen into the 'world'."[2] In falling, Dasein loses itself in "the One," spreading itself over the emptiness—idle talk, curiosity, and ambiguity—of the public domain.

Now, correlating this concept of everyday Dasein with the anonymity characteristic of mythic existence entails two problems. The first concerns the inauthenticity of falling, the second concerns the unidentifiable character—the nobody or nothing—that describes the who of everyday Dasein. As regards the latter issue, rather than losing itself in the namelessness of pure publicness, mythic Dasein "finds" itself identified with specific culture heroes or divine figures. The anonymity of mythic existence does not consist, therefore, in the vagueness of an unidentifiable who—-for example, *das Man.* Rather, the anonymous character of myth derives from the *atemporality* (hence ubiquity) of its sacred referent—*in illo tempore, ab origine*— a referent that is represented in each and every ritual present.

Furthermore, because myth lacks awareness of the isolated singularity of a self on its own as an "I," mythic anonymity, rather than an inauthentic flight in the face of oneself, appears to be a *prepersonal* event whereby Dasein recovers the powerful yet ambiguous ground of its own finite existence. Let us consider this point in greater detail.

---

[2]Ibid., 220.

The originality as well as radicality of Merleau-Ponty's thought lies in his disclosure of the body-subject. With this discovery he succeeded in describing an intentionality that is not simply a function of consciousness, as it was for Kant and the early Husserl. On the contrary, there is the operative intentionality of the body proper, more original than any conscious intentionality of act. Quoting the later Husserl, Merleau-Ponty calls this *fungierende Intentionalität,* "that which produces the natural and antepredicative unity of the world and of our life."[3] In another context Merleau-Ponty refers to this as the "motor power" or "motor intentionality" of the body.[4]

Now, Merleau-Ponty's discussion here has significant implications for the modern problems of subjectivity as well as our present consideration of the who of mythic Dasein. For if consciousness is considered to be the seat of personal (subjective) identity—as has been the tradition since Descartes—then to suggest that subjectivity resides first and foremost in the preconscious intentionality of the body is to suggest that subjectivity is fundamentally prepersonal or anonymous. Indeed, Merleau-Ponty himself uses the impersonal pronoun *on* ("One" or "anonymous existence") in describing this prepersonal subjectivity of the body.[5] I want to argue that we find the source of mythic anonymity, the powerful ground of the myth-making experience, precisely in this *prepersonal,* anonymous subjectivity.

Thus while there may be a superficial resemblance between the anonymity of mythic Dasein and the public anonymity of everyday being-with-one-another, we must not simply assume that such a resemblance indicates an identity. Indeed, on the basis of Heidegger's now well-known interpretation of everyday Dasein, we might be tempted to admit such an identity in order to facilitate our own analysis of mythic existence. For our preunderstanding to be determined

---

[3]Merleau-Ponty, *Phenomenology of Perception,* xviii.

[4]Ibid., 110.

[5]Describing this prepersonal subjectivity of the body, Merleau-Ponty writes, "La perception est toujours dans le mode du 'On'," or again, "Toute perception a quelque chose d'anonyme" *Phénoménologie de la perception* (Paris: Gallimard, 1945) 277, 275. See also Merleau Ponty, *Phenomenology of Perception,* 240, 238.

in advance on the basis of Heidegger's analysis, however, would be not only too easy but possibly also disadvantageous.

Furthermore, we should note that a form of everydayness seems clearly discernible within nonliterate societies as well. This point is illustrated by Raymond Firth's remarks in "Rumor in a Primitive Society," which reflect an analysis of data from a Polynesian island in the Western Pacific. "The Tikopia make no clear-cut categorical distinction between news of verified, accurate type and rumour, unverified and often inaccurate. But indication of some difference is often given by the expression *a taranga o faoa,* meaning 'speech of the crowd' or 'speech of people in general', or by the introductory phrase 'E ati' ... ,'It is held that' ... "[6] Such expressions do not seem to be used by these people, however, with reference to stories that they consider sacred mythic narrations.[7] Thus while everydayness in the form of "idle chatter" appears to exist among nonliterate tribes, it would not be to our advantage to investigate these expressions of *rumor* or everyday being-with-one-another in an attempt to discover the who of mythic Dasein. Rather, we must press forward in securing an original conceptual foundation for our analysis of mythic existence and the ground of the myth-making experience.

A PRELIMINARY CONCEPTION OF DASEIN AS MYTH MAKER

Having laid the foundations for an approach to mythic existence we are now ready to begin analyzing the being of mythic Dasein. Before proceeding, however, we must first offer a preliminary conception of mythic being-in-the-world. As with Heidegger's inquiry concerning the meaning of Being in general, so with our present questioning of the meaning of the Being of myth, various dimensions of the question must be considered in advance.

First, every inquiry is about something, *sein Gefragtes.* Second, there is "that which is to be found out in the asking," *das Erfragte.* Finally, there is "that which is interrogated," or "of whom" the question is asked, *ein Befragtes.*[8] As regards the first, we are evidently in-

---

[6]Raymond Firth, *Tikopia Ritual and Belief* (Boston: Beacon, 1968) 143.

[7]Ibid., also see 284ff.

[8]Heidegger, *Being and Time,* 24.

quiring about the Being of myth, or the nature of mythic Dasein. That which is to be discovered in this case is the structure of mythic existence and the ground of the myth-making experience. Finally, we must decide "of whom" we are asking this question. That is, who or what is to be interrogated in our search for the meaning of mythic being? Obviously, we are asking the question of Dasein *as* myth maker. Again, as with the question of the meaning of Being in general, the question concerning the meaning of myth as an existential possibility can be addressed only to Dasein itself, that is, to the being for whom its very being as a possibility is at stake. Still, who is Dasein as myth maker, and where do we find the mythic mode of being manifesting itself most clearly and unambiguously within culture?

At this point we seem to have entered upon a vicious circle. On the one hand we are striving to discern the structure of myth as an existential possibility of Dasein. On the other hand we need to have a preliminary conception of "who" mythic Dasein is in order to question it further about the structure and meaning of its being-in-the-world. As Heidegger notes regarding any process of questioning, however, "*if we see this circle as a vicious one and look out for ways of avoiding it, even if we just 'sense' it as an inevitable imperfection, then the act of understanding has been misunderstood from the ground up.*"[9] Indeed we must realize that this circle is not vicious; rather, within it "is hidden a positive possibility of the most primordial kind of knowing."[10] Heidegger assures us that "what is decisive is not to get out of the circle but to come into it in the right way. This circle of understanding is . . . [itself] the expression of the existential *fore-structure* of Dasein."[11] Still, what does Heidegger mean by coming into the circle in the right way? Furthermore, what does it mean to say that this circle represents the existential forestructure of Dasein itself? Most simply, it means that understanding is a circular process that proceeds through the interpretive reappropriation of one's preunderstanding. That is, one must be guided in the initial approach to any phenomenon under investigation (for example, myth) by the

---

[9]Ibid., 194.

[10]Ibid., 195.

[11]Ibid.

very forestructure of understanding. We must realize, for example, that our preliminary conception of "whom" we are interrogating about myth does give us some genuine access to the phenomenon. Heidegger warns, however, that "our first, last and constant task is never to allow our . . . fore-conception[s] to be presented to us by fancies and popular conceptions, but rather to make the scientific theme secure by working out these fore-structures in terms of the things themselves."[12]

In view of Heidegger's suggestions, I must now clarify my own preconception of the "who" that is under interrogation when I ask about mythic existence. Furthermore, I must attempt to demonstrate how I arrived at my preunderstanding of Dasein as mythmaker.

In chapter 2, I sought to articulate a concept of embodied subjectivity that adequately reflected the fundamental constitution of being-in-the-world in terms of those elements disclosed in Chapter One— openness, subjectivity, language, and the body. I refused, as Heidegger would say, to be guided in my investigations by "fancies and popular conceptions," seeking rather to secure a solid foundation in terms of the things themselves. With this task in view, I uncovered the primordial linguisticality of human dwelling, concluding that the body is subject as openness-to-world-that-embodies-itself-in-language.

Only after these preliminary investigations did I turn to address some concrete issues that emerged in view of two possible avenues for human linguisticality, speaking and writing. In this regard, I took my clue from purely descriptive accounts of the distinctions associated with the shift from an oral to a written technology of communication. In terms of these descriptions, it became evident that the "transformations of the word affect the total situation of man in the world."[13] Indeed, such a conclusion was quite understandable in view of what our ontological investigations had previously disclosed about the connection between the body, gesture, and speech in the meaningful constitution of being-in-the-world.

In chapter 3 I suggested, finally, that in orally dominated cultures one discovers a unique synthesis of experience and thus an implicit

---

[12]Ibid.

[13]Ong, *The Presence,* 176.

understanding of existence that may be described as "mythical." Indeed, oral traditions seem to manifest a preponderance of what I have prejudicially called mythic modes of experience or involvement with the world. These include a recognition of the sacrality and power of the spoken word; a strong sense of intimacy (preconscious intentional involvement) between body, self, and world; and finally a tendency toward identification with divine heroes as re-presented in oral celebration and ritual reenactment.

Consequently I suggest that the being under investigation in any inquiry concerning the meaning of myth, namely Dasein *as* myth maker, is none other than "premodern Dasein," if by this phrase we mean the mode of being that is intimately connected with speech and is therefore a fundamental possibility for every human existent, "primitive" or otherwise. In this case, expressions of mythic being-in-the-world can be discerned within purely modern cultures insofar as "literate" Dasein not only reads and writes but also speaks and hears (and therefore synthesizes its experience in a more than simply visual, objectivized manner). Inasmuch as those syntheses that I see as productive of the myth-making experience are more prevalent in orally aurally dominated societies, however, I argue that within these cultures mythic Dasein discloses itself in a relatively unadulterated and pristine form. Accordingly, I maintain that nonliterate societies, peoples that have commonly been identified by the term "primitive" must be of central concern if one is to discern the structure of mythic being in its most primordial and definitive expression. I should note, however, that in this category of the nonliterate I include early or marginally literate peoples as well as nonliterate subcultures within literate societies, that is, human groups that still depend heavily upon spoken technologies of communication or are relatively close to vital oral traditions.

Now, it is evident that the social scientific disciplines of ethnography, archeology, and anthropology have offered a plethora of material on nonliterate cultures. While the studies conducted by these disciplines may in fact be suspect on the basis of their ontologically inadequate starting point,[14] it is imperative nevertheless to refer at

---

[14]See Heidegger, *Being and Time,* 76.

least in an illustrative fashion to the data that these disciplines have made available. As Heidegger himself notes,

> Since the positive sciences neither "can" nor should wait for the ontological labours of philosophy to be done, the further course of research will not take the form of an "advance" ... but will be accomplished by *recapitulating* what has already been ontically discovered, and by purifying it in a way which is ontologically more transparent.[15]

I must say, however, that any use of actual ethnographic or anthropological fieldwork is not intended as a way of empirically validating or verifying my ontological descriptions. Indeed, such validation would be impossible if we take Heidegger seriously when he argues that "ethnology itself already presupposes as its clue an inadequate analytic of Dasein."[16]

Unlike Eliade, then, I do not see my project as exercise in comparative history of religions. I do not begin with a descriptive comparison and typology of diverse and disparate ethnographic facts. Accordingly, my work is not open to the sort of criticisms that anthropologists like Edmund Leach have leveled against Eliade's approach, namely, that he constructs his comparative typologies "in a Frazerian fashion, by any snippets of exotic ethnography which conveniently come to hand."[17] On the contrary, my generalizations about myth-making Dasein and the structure of mythic existence do not arise from a simple comparison of ontic or ethnographic facts. Rather, these generalizations are akin to what Heidegger calls "Existentiale,"

---

[15]Ibid., see also my Introduction, 16.

[16]Ibid. Again in this regard, and I cannot emphasize this point too much, while I must take the myths and rituals seriously in conducting a hermeneutical analysis, I must always treat the anthropological interpretations with reservation. Moreover, I must also remember that the myth-ritual data are themselves already interpreted and thus are suspect and may be used, in the final analysis, only in an illustrative manner.

[17]Edmund Leach, "Sermons from a Man on a Ladder," a review of *Mephistopheles and the Androgyne,* by M. Eliade, *New York Review of Books* (October 20, 1966) 28.

and they emerge directly from my earlier analyses of the fundamental structure of Dasein qua embodied subjectivity. In this regard, the ethnographic and anthropological material serve only an illustrative function. Their legitimacy or illegitimacy according to the canons of their own disciplines neither strengthens nor weakens my position here.

Chapter Five

Fundamental Analysis
of Mythic Existence

Having begun with an analysis of man qua Dasein, I shall now consider the nature of Dasein *as* myth maker. My goal here is to demonstrate that the expanded concept of embodied subjectivity developed above is a description of human existence offering genuine access to myth as a primordial mode of being-in-the-world. The uniqueness of this existence rests, I will suggest, in the fact that mythic-Dasein is determined throughout by the phenomenon of *thrownness,* how it finds itself in the world.

In accordance with my discussion about the preliminary conception of Dasein as myth maker, it should be understood that in speaking of mythic Dasein or of myth-making existence, I am referring to the mode of being that is found principally among nonliterate peoples, including contemporary nonliterate tribes as well as pre- and early literate cultures, namely societies dominated by spoken technologies of communication and oral traditions.

INTENTIONALITY AND POWER:
How Mythic Dasein Finds Itself in the World

Following Heidegger's procedure in *Being and Time,* we must proceed here hermeneutically. I will begin with what I presume to be expressions of mythic existence. By interpreting the language and gestures of these expressions in light of the ontological categories developed above, I hope to be able to "tease out" the underlying structures of mythic being-in-the-world.

I start with the assumption that the myth maker qua existing can be no different from any other Dasein. As an embodied subject he finds himself already thrown into a world, drawn toward things, with others, and projected into various situations. Let us take one example:

> The pre-European Tangu were hunters, gardeners, and gatherers. They built thatch-roofed houses of wood on stilts in clearings in the bush. Each year in new gardens each household cultivated yams, bananas, sugarcane and tobacco. They hunted pigs, cassowaries, and lizards, and they gathered a variety of edible wild leaves, fruits and nuts.[1]

Such concrete involvement with the world is illustrated as well in the narrative accounts of the myth maker's heroic ancestors. The myths of the Mardudjara aborigines in Australia, for example, "detail the many exploits of the Dreamtime heroes: their encounters with others, their hunting and gathering, and their naming and creation of the many sites they visited."[2] In any event, human existence is always thrust into a world where it finds itself engaged in various situations and with other people there.

I argue, however that for myth-making existence the *facticity* or *event* of "having been" thrown seems to dominate its experience of being-in-the-world—to such a degree in fact that the myth maker is overwhelmed by his environment. Indeed, mythic Dasein is so powerfully determined by its own thrownness that existence is meaningfully constituted only in the event of identifying oneself with the world. Even a cursory survey of those mythic identifications found in various nonliterate cultures should reveal that myth-making Dasein is overdetermined by that situation in which it already *finds itself* given over. Among numerous examples that could be cited at this point, I would simply remind the reader of the various totemic identifica-

---

[1] Sam Gill, *Beyond "The Primitive": The Religions of Nonliterate Peoples* (Englewood Cliffs NJ: Prentice-Hall, 1982) 9.

[2] Robert Tonkinson, *The Mardudjara Aborigines: Living the Dream in Australia's Desert* (New York: Holt, Rinehart and Winston, 1978) 89.

tions in terms of which tribal societies understand their very existence within the world.

Even ethnographic research illustrates that, with respect to his myth-making activities, nonliterate Dasein has not yet thematized the world as something wholly other than itself. The myth maker does not appear to make radical distinctions between external reality and his own life, between himself and his world. The Melanesian, for example, finds it extremely difficult at times to disengage himself from the world. He does not seem to dissociate his body from his natural, social, and cosmic environment.[3] As W. E. H. Stanner has suggested in his 1953 article "The Dreaming" of the Australian aborigines, "there are many ... such 'onenesses' which I believe I could substantiate. [An aborigine] may 'see' as 'a unity' two persons, such as two siblings or a grandparent and a grandchild; or a living man and something inanimate, as when he tells you that, say, the wollybutt tree, a totem, *is* his wife's brother."[4]

Now, I would contend on purely phenomenological grounds that such overdetermination by facticity, culminating in radical experience of unity or nondissociation between "self" (body-subject) and "world" in myth-making experience, is a function of the Stimmung that is achieved naturally within an orally-aurally dominated world. Recall, for example, our discussion of sound as dynamic, powerful, and enveloping. We find, accordingly, a capacity in audition to synthesize experience in a holistic manner. Hearing thus gives us the situation "in the round," locating the hearer within a total context of aural relations, producing a "sense of unity working out from the world of sound to all actuality."[5] We might say the power of our situated existence discloses itself most dramatically in a world of sound. So predominant is this contextualizing and integrating capacity of sound that "auditory syntheses overwhelm me with phenomena beyond all control."[6] Maurice Leenhardt expresses this idea more concretely when

---

[3]See, e.g., Maurice Leenhardt, *Do Kamo,* trans. B. Miller Gulati (Chicago: University of Chicago Press, 1979) 175, 22.

[4]W. E. H. Stanner, *White Man Got No Dreaming: Essays, 1938-1973* (Canberra: Australia National University Press, 1979) 25.

[5]See above, Chapter 3.

[6]Ong, *The Presence,* 130.

he states, in reference to contemporary nonliterate tribes in Austro-Melanesia, that they live "indeterminate in the envelopment" of their world.[7]

I am suggesting that this sense of envelopment—of being overwhelmed by phenomena and unable to distinguish between one's self and one's world—is grounded in the myth maker's basically auditory way of dealing with the world. The capacity of sound and audition to integrate experience in this way, however, is itself intimately bound up with the ontological connection between speaking and the *openness* of embodied subjectivity in the meaningful constitution of being-in-the-world.

On the other hand, and again like each and every Dasein, the myth maker is not simply there as a presence within the world; he is a subject as well. As an embodied subject, he is the position and state of an intentional existence. Even the stories about his mythological ancestors acknowledge this projective dimension of the myth maker's concrete engagements within the world. For the Australian aborigines, for example, the acts of their Dreamtime heroes are intentional, "as when ... they dig for water and thus create a major waterhole."[8] Again, take the example of Coyote, a mythological trickster figure among the Apache of Southwest America. "Coyote went to the wild mulberry bush. He said to it, 'I want to make a bow. *The people who come after me will make it as I do.*' He got the wood. He cut it off with flint. He split it. Then he whittled it into a bow shape."[9] The Apache, like Coyote in the myth, do just as he did when they want to construct their own weapons today.

As a subject, then, the myth maker projects himself into the world, discovering, creating, and performing meaningful acts. In sum, he endeavors to orient himself in the midst of his surroundings. This effort is evident, for example, in man's early preoccupation with ritual acts and gestures, his constant concern for rites of passage and intiation, ceremonies of renewal, sacralization, and cure. Indeed, the potential orientations in space and time offered by these rites are of such cru-

---

[7]Leenhardt, *Do Kamo,* 60.

[8]Tonkinson, *Mardudjara Aborigines,* 89.

[9]Gill, *Beyond "The Primitive,"* 70.

cial importance in effectively situating man that, "in Caledonia," for example, "yam farming requires approximately eight days of rites for each day of work."[10]

It would be easy to show, furthermore, that all significant activities, from hunting, fishing, and farming to building, dwelling, and dying, are surrounded with similar ritual processes and ceremonies. In virtually all instances such rites perform one common function: by projecting the individual into his surroundings, they serve to orient him meaningfully within his world by creating that orientation *in concreto*. As an intentional subject, then, mythic Dasein seeks order and orientation within the world.

Take, as a more comprehensive example, the following characterization of initiatory rites of passage among the Australian aborigines. These are highly condensed, multidimensional events of cosmic and existential orientation. (1) They are *religious* rites that bring the young man into the spiritual life of the tribe. Being shown, as well as participating in the mysteries of the cult, the novice finds his place within the sacred oral traditions. (2) They are *social* rites of acculturation that transform the youth into a functioning member of the community. He is now able to serve the group by performing economically productive tasks, thereby realizing a new social status. (3) They are rites of *sexual* maturation as well, usually taking place on or about the time of puberty. Often accompanied by circumcision or subincision, the rites serve to initiate the youth into the adult world of marriage and sexual potency. (4) They are also, in this respect, rites of *psychological* maturation. The child becomes an adult. Indeed, the initiate undergoes a death and rebirth ceremony by means of which he secures a completely new personality. The old identity, his previous name, and familial ties to his mother and childhood friends are all forsaken in favor of the new position bestowed upon him. The initiation demands of the youth that he think and respond as a new person. (5) The *dramatic-theatrical* character of the rites is also of critical importance: it gives shape, direction, and efficacy to the initiation proper. Indeed, within the rites, all participants are engaged as actors

---

[10]Leenhardt, *Do Kamo,* 80. Also see M. Young, ed., *The Ethnography of Malinowski* (London: Routledge and Kegan Paul, 1979) 56-58.

in a genuine drama—a drama of cosmic recreation and existential orientation.[11]

Such ritualized existence dramatically exhibits that underlying thrust toward a meaningful orientation within the world. Yet even prior to any conscious deliberation or activity, mythic Dasein is meaning-oriented: the natural motility of his body-as-subject is already intentional and world directed. His body spontaneously moves out into the world, in search of shelter, food, and companionship. In this momentum to exist, the myth maker experiences his body as an opening-on and in-line of his projective field, the focal point of his orientation within the cosmos.

Each ritual act and gesture—indeed, every conscious involvement in the life-world—finds its ground in that preconscious intentional posture of the body-subject's relation to its natural horizon. "The movement upwards as a direction in physical space, and that of desire towards its objective . . . both express the same essential structure of his [being], being situated in relation to an environment."[12] Lacking the precise differentiations that characterize the reflective intentionality of consciousness, the preconscious intentionality of the body-subject succeeds in bringing the whole world into each of its meaningful orientations.[13]

Thus all efforts to secure shelter and obtain food, to gain companionship and establish community, are neither disjunctive areas of a scattered concern nor affairs related simply in terms of external casuality, that is, where one such concern is the effective cause of another. Rather, all such projects and concerns are so many interdependent modalities of the *intentional arc* that extends across and envelops the existential field, which is the vitality of human directedness and situates Dasein in all respects. This power at the root of man's being, this momentum to exist, is the very ground of his meaning-intending existence.

---

[11]See, e.g., Victor Turner, *Dramas, Fields, and Metaphors* (Ithaca: Cornell University Press, 1974) 196-97.

[12]Merleau-Ponty, *Phenomenology of Perception,* 286. Also see Thomas Langan, *Merleau-Ponty's Critique of Reason* (New Haven: Yale University Press, 1966) 51.

[13]See Leenhardt, *Do Kamo,* 60.

If existence is essentially intentional, a movement toward meaning, and if intentionality is originally a preconscious *pouvoir*, that is, an ability to be, a capacity or potentiality to do;[14] indeed, if it is Dasein's *power* of being-in-the-world as such; and if this power is the *potency* of his movements, his *capacity* for speech, and the ground of his orientation within the cosmos—then Van der Leeuw was not wrong when he found that the essence of "religion"—the core of mythic Dasein's concern for meaning and orientation—resides originally in *Power,* in its *mystery* and its control.[15] Existence is Power. Initially it is Dasein's power of movement and speech. Still, this is not simply the power by which one voluntarily gestures in order to realize a specific determination of his will. Rather it is a power that is already there before one, through which one finds oneself existing, already thrown, *able* to move and speak, directed and under way.

For myth-making Dasein, the power of being is thus not personal but *prepersonal.*

> He feels that his own life is dependent upon and supported by the environmental power. But in his eyes it is *not merely the environment,* since this concept presupposes an attitude of disinterested observation which is absolutely foreign to ... the primitive mind; rather is it the very centre of his life. Just as man and tree grow up together, so in ancient Egypt life fluctuates with the rise and fall of the flood waters.[16]

Alternatively, as Leenhardt writes concerning the Canaque, "an identity of substance causes [body and plant] ... to mingle in the same flow of life. ... The human body is composed of that [same] substance which turns green in jade, gives form to foliage, swells every living thing with sap and bursts out in shoots and in the eternal youth of new generations."[17] Man is not the creator of power, but its creature. Whether it be called mana, wakanda, orenda, manitu, petara, hamingja, baraka, sa, tapas, tao, fate, or luck, man always finds him-

---

[14]Kwant, *Phenomenological Philosophy,* 156. Also see Merleau-Ponty, *Phenomenology of Perception,* 137.

[15]See, e.g., Van der Leeuw, *Religion in Essence,* vol. 1.

[16]Ibid., 59.

[17]Leenhardt, *Do Kamo,* 20-21.

self immersed in power, in the midst of it, partaking of it solely by virtue of his embodied being-*there.* "In this light, the whole existence of things and the activity of mankind seem to be embedded, so to speak, in a mythical 'field of force', an atmosphere of potency which permeates everything, and which may appear in concentrated form in certain extraordinary objects."[18] Originally, then, man finds himself always already imbued with power, under its influence, confronted by it, or seeking it out. In any case, he discovers it as something that precedes his own conscious, volitional life.

In these engagements with power, where myth-making Dasein senses the overwhelming presence of phenomena, the preconscious intentional relation between body-as-subject and world-as-lived by the body is making itself felt within his concrete experience. Indeed, the prepersonal integrity of the lived body-world in its intentional structure is meaningful and is initially experienced by Dasein as so many engagements with power.

Furthermore, such experiences of power are the source of mythic anonymity, the locus of the "who" of myth-making Dasein. Mythic identity does not reside in an experience of personal selfhood in the Cartesian sense. Rather the "self" of mythic Dasein is a function of that strong feeling of prepersonal power (*l'On*) in which one participates and that, for this reason, is not strictly speaking one's own. Indeed, the pouvoir or preconscious potentiality of the body-subject is the source of mythic anonymity/identity and comes to the fore as the Power of the life-world, giving to Dasein's relations with that world their depth, their meaning, and their awe-inspiring significance.

At this point we must examine the oral-aural dimensions that semantic field associated with the term "intentionality," and thus the significance of "hearing" or "attending to" something as a precondition for the mythic experience of power. The noun, "intentionality," whose Latin root is still contained in the German *Intentionalität,* is related to the Latin *tendo, tendere,* or the French *tendre. Tendere,* or *tendre,* means "to stretch, strain, extend, lean towards, hold out or offer." *Tendre l'oreille* means "to lend an ear." *Intendo* means "to direct toward" or even "to attend to." As the French verb *entendre* suggests, to intend is first of all "to hear."

---

[18]Ernst Cassirer, *Language and Myth* (New York: Dover, 1953) 63.

Now, if this loosely etymological analysis is applied to some activity on the part of an intentional agent, then this activity will apparently have the following character. The act of intending would itself be first and foremost a *response* to what is heard or *attended to*. Leenhardt relates the following story from Melanesia.

> One commonly hears the story of a young man going into a forest to find the ancestral tree or another tree of the same species. He throws his ax at the trunk and it doesn't catch. "This is neither my father nor my mother," he says. So he goes on to a similar tree. He balances his ax and swings it. It holds in the trunk. *He hears* a man's voice coming out of the tree: "Are you my younger brother?"
>
> "Yes," he replies, "I came to call you. *I want you to make me a house.*"[19]

It appears, then, that the mythic experience of power is a matter of "hearing," "attending," or being "open to" that which *engages* one in the thrown-projection of one's existence.

The myth maker thus finds that power, his power to exist, the power of being itself, is not really within himself, nor even wholly unrelated to him. Rather it is encountered in those locations where the world engages man,—where, in tension with the world, he is *confronted, questioned,* and *called to respond.* Pouvoir, intentionality, motility, or power: whatever it is called, it is experienced precisely at the locations of existential engagement. But where and when does man find himself engaged within the world, confronted with power and called to respond?

The history of religions tells us that almost anything and anyplace can become a hierophany, an engagement with power, a revelation of the sacred, a location of hearing (openness) and response. In short, "it is not a matter of 'what', but of 'how': *not the object of attention, but the sort of attention directed to it.*"[20] What is certain, however, is that, wherever such a hierophany occurs, man's *existential orientation,* his situated being in the world is at stake. If we consider briefly the mythic story related above, for example, we could say that one observes the *attentiveness* or *openness* of existence, and the resultant experience of power, in this simple but *typical* encoun-

---

[19]Leenhardt, *Do Kamo,* 18.

[20]Cassirer, *Language and Myth,* 66.

ter between man and tree. Why this particular tree? Because it is the
first to be felled for the building of a young man's home. Surely the
construction of a dwelling place is the central act of becoming situated for an embodied being-in-the-world. Thus Dasein's engagement
with mythic-power is always matter of "life stances" and "life crises,"[21]
always a matter of orientation.

Is it the sky, the sun or the moon, the passing of the seasons, a
particular tree, stone, or bush, or an animal, natural force, or social
custom in which man feels the pressure of existence, the close proximity of his world, and the call for a confrontation with power? As
Mircea Eliade comments in his *Patterns in Comparative Religion,*

> we must get used to ... recognizing hierophanies absolutely every-
> where, in every area of psychological, economic, spiritual and social
> life. Indeed, we cannot be sure that there is anything—object, move-
> ment, psychological function, being, or even game—that has not at
> some time in human history been somewhere transformed into a
> hierophany. It is quite certain that anything man has ever handled,
> felt, come into contact with or loved can become a hierophany.[22]

Any aspect of his existence has the potential suddenly to capture
man's attention and therewith to become an occasion for an engagement with power, a manifestation of deity, a location of cosmic and
existential orientation.

In the most archaic of cultures, for example, man senses his own finitude in the bounded scope of his vision and the limited reach of his
grasp when, beyond and above him, he confronts the unbounded depth
and height of apparently infinite space. The *vault of heaven,* man's ul-
timate spatial horizon, for this reason has never ceased to draw his attention to that enveloping and awe-inspiring power that its presence
exerts upon him. This has been true even until the present day. Consider the following reflection by a contemporary phenomenologist.

> When I abandon myself to the contemplation of the infinite blue ex-
> panse of the sky ... its existence is in no way that of an intellectual
> object ... but *a living sensible whole,* a 'milieu of a certain vital vi-
> bration which my body adopts.' Since the vibration referred to is the

---

[21]Turner, *Dramas, Fields,* 64.

[22]Mircea Eliade, *Patterns in Comparative Religion,* trans. R. Sheed (New
York: Meridian, 1963) 11.

perceived reality itself, we might best say of the perceived sky, *il se pense en moi*—it thinks itself in me.[23]

Certainly, this reflection underscores the dynamic reciprocity between body-subject and world, wherein the event of *attending* or *being open* to something succeeds in disclosing a "living sensible whole," a power that exerts its vitality upon me and to which my body responds. Such a reflection ends by saying no more and no less than myth says in the same situation: *il se pense en moi.*

The heavenly bodies as well have, since man's beginning, revealed that ubiquitous bond between man and world in which the power of existence bares itself.

> Many savages, on seeing the new moon for the first time in [the month,] observe ceremonies which seem to be intended to renew and increase their life and strength with the renewal and increase of the lunar light. . . . For example, on the day when the new moon first appeared, the Indians of San Juan Capistrano in California used to call together all the young men and make them run about, while the old men danced in a circle saying, 'As the old moon dieth and cometh to life again, so we also having to die will live again'. . . . Others in the Congo say, 'so may I renew my life as thou art renewed'.[24]

These various stories, beliefs, incantations, and ceremonies—as responses to man's experience of power—illustrate the intimate bond between man and world. In this respect, they are significant for man's orientation within the world, ordering his cosmos and locating him meaningfully in its midst.

Other such hierophanies occur with the gathering or hunting of food, in matters of kinship organization and social communion, in problems of sexual maturation, desire, anxiety, and love. In every modality of existence, the mysterious power of man's being-*there* confronts him: that *intentional arc* makes itself felt at those locations of his engagement with the world. In every instance, this advent of power serves to further man's sense of belonging to the whole of things.

---

[23]Langan, *Merleau-Ponty's Critique,* 31-32.

[24]James George Frazer, *The Belief in Immortality* (London: 1913) 68. See also Benjamin Ray, "Death, Kingship, and Royal Ancestors in Buganda, " in F. Reynolds and E. Waugh, eds., *Religious Encounters with Death* (University Park: Pennsylvania State University Press, 1977) 63-64.

I would suggest, in conclusion, that the myth-making experience and the "who" of mythic Dasein are grounded in the *how* of primordial embodied subjectivity: (1) in the *felt intimacy* of body-subject and world, manifesting itself in experiences of radical engagement with Power; (2) in the *efficacy* and *vitality* of the spoken word as the concrete embodiment of Dasein's openness to world and thus finally; (3) in that predominantly auditory synthesis, or Stimmung, on the basis of which the various modalities of existence are lived in an original form of complex interdependence.

Recall again my example of the initiation rites in aboriginal Australia, rites in which religious, social, economic, sexual, psychological, and aesthetic dimensions of existence are all condensed into one highly compact and thus symbolic set of events. Alternatively, think of the traditional figure of the shaman.[25] He functions simultaneously as priest, doctor, spiritual guide, political and economic adviser prophet, and also as dramatis persona. His projects permeate every aspect in the communal life of the tribe. His gestures and incantations bespeak a dense and highly volatile cosmos, whose dimensional compactness reveals the myth maker's preobjective sense of being in the world and the fundamental pouvoir that he concretely experiences as Power.

In myth-making experience, the lived body-world is a compact consubstantial whole, in which all regional concerns mutually embrace and reciprocally constitute one another, orienting Dasein in the whole current of life. Here one observes the various modalities of existence lived as a complex engagement with Power, with the power of being itself. In the following section, I shall consider the way in which this powerful and dimensionally compact experience of myth-making Dasein is taken up and articulated within the compact logos of mythic discourse.

THE STRUCTURE OF MYTHIC DISCOURSE:
A Powerful and Compact Word

In my introduction, I indicated that myth is the primordial event of human linguisticality, giving Dasein its first orientation within the world.

---

[25]See, e.g., Eliade, *Shamanism*, Bollingen Series (Princeton: Princeton University Press, 1972).

If embodied subjectivity has come to mean that the body is subject that embodies itself in language, however, then myth (as a linguistic event) is the embodiment of a particular mode of being-in-the-world, grounded in a unique experience of facticity. Indeed, if myth intends a world, and if the world of its meaning is the originally powerful and compact lived body-world structure of myth-making experience, then mythic discourse is a powerful and compact logos: somewhat opaque and highly symbolic. By symbolic, I mean simply that mythic images are pregnant with significance, displaying that "functional economy" at work in all aspects of mythic existence.[26] It is necessary at this point to describe the structure of relations between the condensed *thickness* of myth-making experience and its concrete embodiment in the compact plurivocality of the mytho-logos.

The uniqueness of mythic existence has been shown to reside in its experience of thrownness as power. This power is neither subjective nor objective. Rather, it is relational, a function of the prepersonal intentionality of embodied subjectivity as it opens itself to the world. It is the source of both mythic anonymity and ritual identity, the "who" of mythic Dasein.

Now, because of its dialectical nature, the experience of power has an ambiguous connection with mythic discourse as the concrete embodiment of mythic existence. On the one hand, it is because of the nature of sound and speech in particular that myth-making Dasein associates power foremost with the spoken word. "Being powered projections spoken words have an aura of power."[27]

On the other hand, the mythic word is also a response of the experience of power. In view of the fundamental structure of embodied subjectivity, mythic Dasein succeeds in articulating this experience only by "speaking-out," giving power a name and therefore a concrete embodiment within the world.

For myth-making Dasein, then, there is the closest connection between the spoken name (or word) and the essence or power of a being. We could say, in fact, that the word-sign "coincides with that which is indicated . . . the sign itself always *is* what it indicates."[28] Stanner

---

[26]Percy Cohen, "Theories of Myth," *Man,* n.s. 4 (1969): 351.

[27]Ong, *The Presence,* 112.

[28]Heidegger, *Being and Time,* 113.

agrees that, for the Australian aborigine, "the name is like an intimate part of the body [of a person], with which another person does not take liberties."[29] Why is this so? Because a person's essence, the power of his being, resides within his name. The word, then, not only names an object or person but effectively embodies its/his power or essence. We must remember, however, that this "coinciding" or embodying of the referent in the word-sign

> is not an identification of things which have hitherto been isolated from each other: it consists rather in the fact that the sign has not yet become free from that of which it is a sign. Such a use of signs is still absorbed completely in Being-towards what is indicated, so that a sign as such cannot detach itself at all. This coinciding is based not on a prior Objectification but on the fact that such Objectification is completely lacking.[30]

We could say, then, that in the myth-making experience of power and its connection with speech there is a celebration of the essential structure of embodied subjectivity, namely of preconscious intentionality embodying itself in the spoken word. In any event, while the mythic word is the source of the experience of power, so too the experience of power gives rise to the word of myth. Within this dialectical and thus ambiguous relation between word and power, we find the source of the opacity of myth. In terms of this opacity we must seek to determine further the structure of mythic discourse as the embodiment of mythic being-in-the-world.

As indicated above, in its earliest expression among nonliterate cultures, the spoken word of myth necessarily precedes those objectivizing consequences of literacy and its accompanying forms of conceptual and speculative abstraction.[31] The mythic word precedes the ontological bifurcation of body-subject and world, as well as the disintegration of the dimensionally compact life-world. Accordingly, myth displays the intentional bonds of a unified existence, giving voice to the power of a compact existential engagement between man and world.

---

[29]Stanner, *White Man,* 25.

[30]Heidegger, *Being and Time,* 113.

[31]See, e.g., Goody, *Domestication,* ch. 1; Ong, *The Presence,* chap. 3.

On the one hand, then, myth is *dimensionally compact.* The utterances of mythic discourse potentially touch upon all aspects of existence, from sex to religion. It is not that each and every myth will speak to or about every possible human concern but rather that, in its dimensional compactness, every myth will disclose various regions of a concerned and engaged being in the world.

This dimensional compactness is one of the sources of the opacity of myth, human significance being "compressed" within its images.[32] If meanings are compressed within mythic images, however, then a plurality of senses is a potentiality grounded in the very structure of myth itself. The *topography* of this plurivocality, however, and the movements between and among its various horizons of potential meaning, are not clearly delineated. As the compact gesture of a compact world, whose various dimensions are so closely knit together, myth does not naturally articulate itself according to the neatly analytical divisions of modern technical research. On these grounds, one might say that violence must be done to the myth in order to elicit its various possible senses.

Still, another, even more fundamental source of opacity acts as a stumbling block to the understanding and interpretation of mythic discourse. Because it undercuts the objectivizing bifurcation of body-subject and world, myth is *ontologically compact* as well. Because of the initial unity of the lived body-world in myth-making experience, Dasein feels the intensity of that bond uniting him with the world that is his intentional correlate. Ontically this is experienced as "the overwhelming proximity of the object, the oneness of man and the world."[33] In view of this situation, myth discloses things within an aura of powerfulness. The density as well as the opacity of myth rests ultimately upon its residing within this aura of power.

The structure of mythic discourse, then, is itself a function of the underlying structure of embodied subjectivity. Mythic Dasein's experience of power finds embodiment in mythic discourse much as the operative intentionality (pouvoir) of the body-subject finds articu-

---

[32]See, e.g, Daniel Guerriere, "The Structure of Mythic Existence," *Personalist* 55 (1974): 261-72.

[33]Merleau-Ponty, *Phenomenology of Perception,* 291.

late embodiment in speech. For this reason, the myth-making experience of power finds its most appropriate medium of self-disclosure in the spoken word.

In order to demonstrate more dramatically the unique relationship between the experience of power and its embodiment in mythic narrative, I turn now to the Babylonian Creation Myth, *Enuma elish,* and its setting in the ancient Near East. I realize of course that the text under consideration at this point is a written document and therefore a product of literate culture. Archeological evidence, however, supports the hypothesis that this is a later recension of earlier documents that probably have their roots within an older oral tradition.[34] Furthermore, certain scholars have noted that this narrative was verbally recited in ancient Babylonia during celebration of the New Year festival.[35] In any event, I have already suggested above that written products of early literate cultures may be considered as belonging to the proper domain of myth-making Dasein insofar as such productions are still relatively close to oral traditions and more predominantly spoken technologies of communication.

Life in ancient Mesopotamia flourished along the alluvial banks of the Tigris and Euphrates rivers. These rivers, flowing down out of the highlands, emptied, at their mouths, into the Persian Gulf. The arable land was formed where the rivers deposited their silt, just above the Gulf waters, creating the marshy, swamplike environment of this part of the fertile crescent. As Henri Frankfort observes, "The lowest course of these two rivers presents a wilderness of reed forests where the [inhabitants] lead an amphibious existence." Indeed, the wet marshes are so much the ground they walk on that the floors of their huts "often ooze water at every step."[36] The country, then, the very land comprising Mesopotamia, was continuously created from the deposits of silt naturally brought down by the "sweet waters" of the Tigris and Euphrates. By such means, the alluvial banks grew, eventually swell-

---

[34]See, e.g., A. Heidel, *The Babylonian Genesis* (Chicago: University of Chicago Press, 1972).

[35]See, e.g., Eliade, *Cosmos and History,* trans. W. Trask (New York: Harper & Row, 1962); *The Symbolism of Evil* (Boston: Beacon, 1969).

[36]Henri Frankfort, *The Birth of Civilization in the Ancient Near East* (New York: Doubleday, 1956) 45.

ing out further into the Gulf, giving birth to new land where there had once been only the salty water of the Ocean.[37] The damp, rich, and fertile soil that was the outcome of this natural process was perfect for an agricultural community, just right for the cultivation of food and the bearing of new life.

This entire process, however, from the depositing of silt by the rivers to the emergence of life-giving earth in the Gulf and its subsequent cultivation by man, was not an uninterrupted and paradisical situation. Indeed, conditions were often very precarious in this wet and stormy land. The environment was not always helpful or even agreeable. The situation was highly unstable throughout the year and therefore unpredictable.

> Sudden changes could bring about conditions beyond man's control. Spring tides in the Persian Gulf may rise to a height of eight to nine feet; prolonged southerly gales may bank up the rivers for as much as two feet or more. Abnormal snowfalls in Armenia, or abnormal rainfall farther south, may cause a sudden rise of level in the rivers; a landslide in the narrow gorges of the two Zabs or of the Khabur may first hold up, then suddenly release, an immense volume of water. Any one of these circumstances . . . may create a flow which the earth embankments of the southern plain are not able to contain,[38]

leaving the inhabitants utterly stranded in a chaotic wasteland of water.

We find, then, that the creative life-producing and sustaining conditions were also destructive and life endangering. Upon them life in ancient Mesopotamia literally depended. If those who inhabited this land were ever attentive or *open to* their life-world in situations demanding a response to the concrete experience of power, it was certainly here in the unpredictable contingencies of their environment. In such engagements with these life-and death-dealing conditions the inhabitants must undoubtedly have realized, in part, an essential reciprocity with their world, the intimacy of their relations to it, the reality of their dependence upon it. Such situations were, par excellence,

---

[37]Henri Frankfort et al., *Before Philosophy* (Baltimore: Penguin, 1972) 185-86.

[38]Frankfort, *The Birth*, 53.

revelatory of the mysterious power of their being-in-the-world: a power already there before them, both creative and destructive, in relation to which they felt they must continually orient themselves. Here, then, the Mesopotamians sought to develop their commerce with the world and its power, a commerce that they prereflectively knew was already established, making simple material and social existence possible.

It is not surprising, therefore, that the divine heroes of the cosmogonic myth, *Enuma elish,* should etymologically mirror the very life-conditions through which the Mesopotamians first experienced the power of their intentional embodiment within the world. We see, in fact, that in the narrative *Apsu* names the god or power of the sweet subterranean waters of the Tigris and Euphrates, projected here back into the time of the origins. *Ti'amat* is the power of the salty seawater of the Persian Gulf. *Mummu,* Apsu's visier, is the power of the mist and cloud banks hanging low over these primeval waters.[39] "Mingling their waters together," Apsu and Ti'amat give birth to *Lahmu* and *Lahamu* and silt and soft mud deposits at the mouths of these rivers as they flow into the waters of the Gulf. As these silt deposits build up, eventually forming an alluvial soil, they give birth to the next pair of deities, *Anshar* and *Kishar,* the male and female aspects of the horizon, the circular rim of heaven and earth. Deposited along the edge of the primeval waters, the newly formed soil *stands out,* itself giving form to the first line of the horizon, distinguishing that which is above (Anshar) from the emerging land below (Kishar). Thus do these two deities anticipate the birth of their own offspring, *Anu,* god of the sky, and *Ea,* god of the earth and marshes.

The partial decoding of names in the first part of the first tablet of the myth by no means constitutes even a preliminary interpretation of the narrative. I am not suggesting, in other words, that the myth is simply an allegorical decription of the way in which new land is formed in the Delta, nor is it to be understood as a prescientific explanation of the origin of the cosmos, again based on man's naive experience of the emergence of new land from a watery chaos. Rather, such etymological decoding seeks only to suggest that, in those vi-

---

[39]Frankfort et al., *Before Philosophy,* 186.

tally pressing relations with his world, feeling the power of embodied existence, Dasein responds with myth. As a response to this experience of the power of existential engagement, myth is an attempt to interpret one's situation, to orient oneself meaningfully in that world in which one finds oneself always already thrown and under way.

Thus, contrary to Max Muller's contention, it is not a disease of language that such cosmogonic heroes etymologically re-present the various conditions of that life-world in which the Mesopotamian finds himself dramatically confronted with the power of his being-there. On the contrary, these linguistic connections between the proper names of the mythic heroes and the ontic realities that they embody disclose those genuine locations of the Mesopotamian's engagement in his world. They tell us where and when he is confronted by the finitude and contingency of embodied existence, how he experiences his potentiality for being and nonbeing.

In fact, as the above analysis of these names affirms, the efficacy of myth lies in its "giving voice" to Dasein's concerned and complex existence within a world with which he is dynamically and powerfully involved. Paul Ricoeur agrees when he states that the symbols of myth "plunge their roots into the durable constellations of life, feeling, and the universe . . . , into the shadowy experience of power."[40] And what else is this experience of power if not the mysterious *openness* of existence itself, of man's standing out into the world—an openness where man is engaged by the world and wherein emerges a place for him to dwell meaningfully?

I should note, furthermore, that such occurrences of existential engagement vary according to the environment and type of setting in which Dasein finds himself thrown and asked to respond. Not simply the natural world but the social, political, economic, and cultural milieu in which he dwells will contribute as well to Dasein's particular encounter with power, to his ontic experience of being as intentional, in which a meaningful orientation is sought and secured. Let us take one example:

The various city gods in whom the earlier settlers [of Mesopotamia]

---

[40]Paul Ricoeur, *Interpretation Theory* (Fort Worth TX: T.C.U. Press, 1976) 64, 69.

trusted appear to be powers in the basic economies characteristic of the region in which their cities were situated. Thus in the south we find a group of city gods closely related to marsh life and its primary economies, fishing and hunting: Enki, god of the fresh water and of vegetable and animal life in Eridu in the west, and in the east, Nanshe, goddess of fish; Dumuzi-abzu, the power of new life in the watery deep; and others in Nina and Kinirsha.[41]

Thus it is not as if the intentional arc were some sort of mechanical force or internal psychic structure acting as the effective cause of social, political, sexual, and economic orientations and so forth. Rather, it is a matter of the reciprocal action of various intentional fields. "Existence is not a set of facts capable of being reduced" one to the other or to some common causal factor. Rather existence is "the ambiguous setting of [the] intercommunication [of all areas of life], the point at which their boundaries run into each-other, or again their woven fabric."[42] The natural, social, sexual, psychological, and economic dimensions are all dialogical modalities of an intentional existence, each one mediating Dasein's movements and projects in all of the other spheres. They all work together in myth, orienting Dasein within the whole setting of his life, wherein morality, religion, nature, society, aesthetics and exchange all come together.

Myth discloses the compact interdependence of all these modalities of life as so many engagements with power, engagements that ultimately define the shape of mythic Dasein's being in the world. This fabric of experience, and its embodiment in the plurivocality of the mythic logos, thus characterize the symbolic structure of myth as discourse.

Now, when interpreting myth, one should keep in mind that the compactness that I described above as a topography of meanings does not imply discrete levels of objective sense or some hierarchy of significations. Rather, all potentially enunciable meanings are so many interrelated features of the mythic topos woven into the very fabric of the narrative structure itself. The primary function of myth is therefore not to represent one region of concern abstractly, objec-

---

[41]Thorkild Jacobsen, *Treasures of Darkness* (New Haven: Yale University Press, 1978) 25.

[42]Merleau-Ponty, *Phenomenology of Perception,* 166.

tively, and independently of all others. Rather its meaning is more comprehensive—singular yet complex. Most generally, we could say that myth has an *existential function*—serving to orient Dasein within the world as a complex yet integrated whole, giving Dasein a purpose or meaning, that is, opening up possibilities for his self-understanding. We could say, therefore, that while *Enuma elish* satisfies this basically existential need of the ancient Mesopotamians for an ordered orientation vis-à-vis the felt powers of existence, it also allows for various aspects of that fundamental existential sense to be articulated as well. Jacobsen and others have attempted to do this in respect to the possible political and psychoanalytical dimensions of the myth.[43] Still, just as this myth is not a naive, protoscientific explanation of the supernatural origins of the universe, so it is not simply an objective account of Marduk's (or any other ruler's) historical accession to political supremacy in the ancient Near East, nor is it merely an objective analysis of the psychological conditions and neuroses underlying the rise of a civilized State. Rather, as myth, it is a pregnant and compact narrative that helped the myth makers articulate their experience of being engaged by and in the midst of their world as a compact and powerful whole. As myth, *Enuma elish* thus brings forth in a common voice the vital forces and concerns of Dasein's concrete existence and its mysterious yet powerful ground.

THE EXISTENTIAL FUNCTION OF MYTH AND ITS RELIGIOUS CHARACTER

In the previous section we were concerned with the structure of mythic discourse (Rede) as a concrete embodiment of mythic existence. In that context we discovered a double compactness at the heart of the mytho-logos, an *ontological* as well as a *dimensional* compactness, corresponding to the *powerful* and *integrated* mythic experience of facticity. Accordingly, we argued that myth displays a fundamental plurivocality, speaking out, in a condensed and therefore somewhat opaque manner, the various dimensions of mythic Dasein's compact existence. In view of this situation, I suggested that myth has a basically existential function, symbolically disclosing the complexity of mythic

---

[43]See, e.g., Jacobsen, *Treasures,* 183-91.

Dasein's engagements within a powerful and integrated cosmos. I will characterize this existential function of myth further.

I referred in an earlier chapter to the referential or apophantic function of language: its capacity to disclose things within the world by pointing them out. In this manner of pointing out, the assertion ultimately opens up a region of objectivities that may be further adumbrated in more technical forms of communication. There is reason to believe, however, that this is neither the original nor the genuine function of language. As Heidegger contends, the authentic and truly creative function of language resides in its capacity to articulate an existential understanding—whereby being-in-the-world as a possibility comes to audition in a distinctively human way.[44] By means of this existential function, or *Seinsverstehen,* we grasp the concrete orientations of a subject embodied within the world in the midst of his daily concerns.

Now, precisely this Seinsverstehen I find to be the central function of myth and the foundation of all potential meanings in the mythic logos. Thus I can agree with Cassirer when he suggests that the unity of myth lies not in its object but only in a "unity of function expressed in a unique mode of experience."[45] I must disagree, however, when, in *The Myth of the State,* he argues that this function is primarily socio-psychological.[46] Indeed, if myth is a response to Dasein's experience of the overwhelming power of his compact existence, then the principal function of mythic discourse is to articulate Dasein's situation vis-à-vis that experience as a whole and its complex integrity. In fact, I argue that the *raison d'être* of myth is to secure for man a total orientation (Seinsverstehen) within that openness (*Lebensraum*) disclosed by the mythic experience of power. Thus, when I said above that *Enuma elish* satisfies the basic need for a fundamental orientation within the cosmos, I meant that uniquely existential function of myth whereby Dasein discovers the various dimensions of his being in the world as a powerful and compact whole. Accordingly, the

---

[44]See Heidegger, *Being and Time,* secs. 31-34.

[45]See, e.g., David Bidney, "Myth, Symbolism, and Truth," in T. Sebeok, ed., *Myth: A Symposium* (Philadelphia: American Folklore Society, 1955) 3.

[46]See Ernst Cassirer, *The Myth of the State* (New Haven: Yale University Press, 1950). Also see Bidney, "Myth," 6-8.

underlying meaning in myth is its *existential* sense, wherein the basic questions of life crisis/orientation are addressed.

Now, if human existence as a whole is the essential concern of myth, then it follows that all those dimensions of meaning that interpreters can extract from the myth proper are so many objectivizations of that comprehensive and originally compact *Seinsverstehen.* They are abstract and somewhat truncated senses, graspable as such only by a critical reading. Thus, the political, psychological, economic, historical, or sociological dimensions are not initially or consciously written into the myth as such and certainly not in any discrete or objective manner. Rather, these alternative dimensions of meaning are basically critical reconstructions, modern adumbrations read into the myth, and are grounded ultimately, not in the myth proper, but in the unique preunderstandings of its various interpreters. For this reason violence must be done to the myth in eliciting the potential meanings.

It does not follow, however, that the plurivocality of myth is merely extrinsic and unrelated to the narrative structure. On the contrary, all such critical readings are granted only on the basis of that original, existential function of the compact mytho-logos. In fact, it is the very nature of myth, in its existential sense, to "give rise to thought"[47] and to stimulate the formulation of various critical dimensions of meaning. In the myth proper, however, what we hear first and foremost is "a piece of self-world being"[48]: bodying forth existence within the word, myth exposes the compact integrity of being-*there* in the world as a powerful whole.

In terms of dimensional compactness, then, the existential function of myth serves to disclose the integrity and multidimensionality of mythic Dasein's orientation within the world. In terms of ontological compactness, on the other hand, the existential function of myth betrays the essential interdependence or identity between its word, its speaker, and what is spoken of. In this regard, we could state that the images of myth "really contain their meaning, which is not a no-

---

[47]See Ricoeur, *Symbolism,* 347-57.

[48]Albert Hofstadter, *Truth and Art* (New York: Columbia University Press, 1965) 71.

tional meaning, but a direction or pulse of existence running through them."[49] For this reason it is difficult to interpret or translate myth by forcing the chiaroscuro character of its existential sense into the unambiguous, univocal, and devitalized categories of an objectivistic thought and language.

For the same reason, the myth maker makes no real distinction between the myth in its appearance (the mythic images), the reality that it calls up or discloses (the presumed referents/events of the mythic recitation), and the mythic power that such events and images embody. Indeed, for the believer, the myth (as well as those events to which it gives voice) is imbued with the potency of the real; it contains the power of being within itself. "The myth holds the essence *within* the appearance; the mythical phenomenon is not a representation, but a genuine presence. The daemon of rain is present in each drop which falls after an incantation," as is the divinity himself present in the person of the ritual actor. "Every apparition is in this case an incarnation," every image the concrete embodiment of what it expresses.[50] The mythic word is bound up with the reality that it discloses: the two are of one substance. For this reason the spoken word of myth wields power, is powerful. "In oral-aural cultures it is thus eminently credible that words can be used to achieve an effect such as weapons or tools can achieve. Saying evil things of another is thought to bring him direct physical harm."[51]

Herein lies the real efficacy of myth and mythico-ritual gestures: myth both discloses and creates the concrete orientation or *Seinsverstehen* of Dasein within a totality of meaning and power. The symbolic structure of mythic narrative is thus a matter of the relations between power and its vocalizations, between intentionality and its dimensionally compact expression.

I have suggested that the dimensional as well as the ontological compactness of the myth-making experience is taken up in the existential function of myth through the powerful and plurivocal tex-

---

[49]Merleau-Ponty, *Phenomenology of Perception,* 285.

[50]Ibid., 290.

[51]Ong, *The Presence,* 113.

ture of its images or symbols. Accordingly, this existential understanding is itself a voice of that concrete intentionality that *is* the dynamic structure of human embodiment. The mythic, then, is extended in two directions, one linguistic and the other nonlinguistic: it "hesitates on the dividing line between *bios* and *logos.*"[52] Facing both ways, myth has a Janus face: it speaks out, in an originary voice, that which is never fully vocalized but which gives speech its existentially expressive power. If language is the expression of a gestural sense, bodying forth existence within the word, mythic discourse is a *semblance* of man's intentional being, literally "bringing together" or "collecting" the various dimensions of his being-in-the-world within a single and compact logos—a logos that *recollects,* in the fullest sense of the word, the ubiquity of the myth maker's experience of Power. In this respect the mythic word is symbolic, disclosing a truly religious significance.

I am not suggesting here that all myths will speak of divine powers or gods and are therefore religious. Rather I am making the claim that all myths are a response to what is experienced as power, that is, to what engages man in his being-in-the-world as an open possibility. Correlatively, I am maintaining that this engagement with power is usually interpreted as a confrontation with what is considered to be holy or the sacred. As Walter Ong suggests "sounds [especially in an aurally dominated culture] . . . tend to assimilate themselves to voices. . . . Moreover, since sound is indicative of here-and-now actuality, the word as sound establishes here-and-now personal presence. . . . As establishing personal presence, the word has immediate religious significance."[53]

As we saw in numerous instances above, the experience of power that lies at the basis of the myth-making experience is, more often than not, interpreted as a hierophany, a personal manifestation of deity—the sacred, the taboo, or the holy. Because of this intimate connection between power and the sacred in human experience, virtually all myths may legitimately be said to have a religious dimension or character. In conclusion, the existential function, or *Seinsverstehen,*

---

[52]Ricoeur, *Interpretation Theory,* 53-54, 59.

[53]Ong, *The Presence,* 131.

of myth itself, rooted in that mysterious power (pouvoir) of existence, discloses the religious significance of the mytho-logos.

> Even before Eliade, Rudolph Otto . . . strongly emphasized the ap-
> pearance of the sacred as power, strength, efficacity. This is valuable
> in that it helps us to be on guard against all attempts to reduce [myth]
> linguistically. We are warned from the very beginning that we are here
> crossing the threshold of an experience that does not allow itself to
> be completely inscribed within the categories of logos. . . . The nu-
> minous element [namely, Power] is not first a question of language,
> if it ever really becomes one, for to speak of power is to speak of
> something other than speech even if it implies the power of speaking.
> This power and efficacity *par excellence* is what does not pass over
> completely into the articulation of meaning.[54]

Rooted in the shadowy experience of power, of the sacred, myth
is involved with an essential opacity, a *mysterium.* It can never make
fully explicit the sacred force or power that binds it to the world and
is the ground of its own power of speaking. As the nonlinguistic pole
of myth, Dasein's rooted transcendence embraces all linguistic senses
of the mytho-logos that is its semblance. Appearing in and *as* what is
disclosed by the mythic symbols, existence conceals its intentional
ground within the panoply of potential meanings. Yet in spite of its
hiddenness, this mysterious power of being is always felt throughout
the narrative itself. The pole of linguistic meanings, grounded as it is
in the existential function of myth, continuously points beyond itself,
or rather, continuously points to its hidden texture. In any case, it always discloses the openness of human existence and those locations
within that existence where intentionality makes itself felt (or heard)
as power, as the power of the Sacred.

Herein lies the genuinely religious character of myth: as a compact *logos,* it "gathers together" into a symbolic whole the entire
spectrum of human experience, disclosing the relations between the
life-world of concrete existence and the essential ground of being as
Power or the Sacred.

---

[54]Ricoeur, *Interpretation Theory,* 60-61.

Chapter Six

Time and Myth

Having analyzed the structure of mythic existence in light of the concept of embodied subjectivity, we must now attempt to disclose "that which makes possible what has been projected" in our analytic. When I speak of a primordial existential interpretation of mythic Dasein, I refer to an analysis disclosing the horizon in view of which mythic existence may be conceived in its possibility as that which it is. Heidegger would call this the meaning (*Sinn*) of mythic Dasein—"that wherein the understandability of [mythic existence] maintains itself."[1]

In *Being and Time* Heidegger demonstrates that temporality is the ontological horizon or meaning of Dasein: it is that which makes possible the structural whole called being-in-the-world. Similarly, I will show that temporality is the meaning of the being of myth—that in terms of which mythic Dasein may be understood in its very ground.

We shall see how the temporal character of myth-making experience reveals human action in terms of "historicity," that is, in the mode of being that Heidegger calls *Wiederholung,* or repetition.[2] I shall demonstrate that such repetition is the ground or meaning of mythic subjectivity. I will effect this demonstration in part through an ex-

---

[1]Heidegger, *Being and Time,* 371, 370.

[2]Paul Ricoeur, "The Human Experience of Time and Narrative," *Research in Phenomenology* 9 (1979): 20.

amination of mythic narrative. My assumption here is that the temporal foundation of myth-making experience finds adequate expression in mythic narration. Such an assumption is partly dictated by my previous discovery of the body-subject embodying itself in language. Together with Paul Ricoeur's claim that "narrativity is the mode of discourse through which the mode of being which we call temporality ... is brought to language,"[3] my discovery suggests that the ground of mythic subjectivity will be adequately grasped through an analysis of the style and plot structure of mythic narration.

I will argue, in this regard, that by returning to and repeating the deeds of a heroic (archetypal) past, mythic narrative enables the believer to recollect those possibilities (in illo tempore, ab origine) that are uniquely and fundamentally his own. In other words, by means of the mythic narrative movement, Dasein effectively comes back to himself—becoming *who he is* through *being who he was*—in the figure of the mythic hero.

TEMPORALITY AS THE ONTOLOGICAL HORIZON
OF THE MEANING OF DASEIN

In division 1 of part 1 of *Being and Time,* Heidegger offers a fundamental analysis of human existence. Within that context he describes the unitary phenomenon of being-in-the-world. Considering various aspects of this structure, we discover that existence (Dasein) is thrown into a world, involved with and concerned about things in its very being-there. In short, Dasein is seen to be characterized by an openness or transcendence toward the world.

Articulating further the openness of Dasein's structure, Heidegger considers three equiprimordial elements: *Befindlichkeit,* or "state of-mind"; *Verstehen,* or "projective understanding"; and *Verfallen,* or "falling." These elements compose the being of the *there.* Describing the constitutive role of the first two of these structural elements, Heidegger writes: "states-of-mind and understanding characterize the primordial disclosedness of Being-in-the-world. By way of having a mood, Dasein 'sees' possibilities in terms of which it is."[4] Those pos-

---

[3]Ibid., 17.

[4]Heidegger, *Being and Time,* 188.

sibilities that Dasein may or may not choose and that are projected by the understanding are grounded in that sense of *how one is situated,* one's state of mind or predisposition. In other words, the projection of possibilities occurs always and only on the basis of one's mood, that place where one is coming from.

Heidegger concludes, accordingly, that Dasein exists as a thrown project. Even at this juncture one can begin to see how temporality will emerge as the ontological horizon or meaning of being, namely that which makes possible Dasein's being-in-the-throw. Indeed, the very image of "being thrown" indicates that Dasein has a whence from which it has come as well as a whither toward which it is going.

Now, as being-in-the-world, Dasein may be described as being "outside-itself," "absorbed-in" its world, "alongside" entities with which it is involved and by means of which it finds itself determined.[5] In its everyday mode of existing, this point was demonstrated through an analysis of the phenomenon of *falling*—an ontological description of Dasein in its being-with the other and under the domination of *das Man.* As falling, Dasein belongs to that world in which it is *present,* determined by that which surrounds it and lays claim to its very being there.

Because this absorption in the world has the fundamental character of being-in-the-throw, however, it follows that Dasein is equiprimordially determined by a "having-been," namely, that *factical* state in which it *already* finds itself thrown, as well as by a "toward-which," that is, those possibilities that are "ahead-of-it" and are disclosed within projective understanding as such. Accordingly, "Dasein's totality of Being as Care means: ahead-of-itself-already-being-in (a world) as Being-alongside (entities encountered within-the-world)."[6]

Such, a description demonstrates quite clearly that temporality is the fundamental horizon or meaning of Dasein as a thrown-project. Indeed, the primordial integrity of this structural whole lies in the unity of its temporal-ecstatic modalities.

The "ahead-of-itself" is grounded in the future. In the "Being-already-

---

[5]See ch. 2.

[6]Heidegger, *Being and Time,* 375.

in . . . ", the character of "having been" is made known. "Being-alongside . . . " becomes possible in making present. . . . Temporality [thus]
makes possible the unity of existence [understanding], facticity
[mood] and falling, and in this way constitutes primordially the totality of the structure of Care.[7]

Temporality, then, is that on the basis of which Dasein's existence
within the world is made possible. Only because it exists as self-temporalizing, disclosing a "for-the-sake-of" (future), an "in-the-face-of-
which" (past), and an "in-order-to" (present), does Dasein exist at all.
"The phenomena of the 'towards . . . .', the 'to . . . .', and the 'alongside
. . . .' make temporality manifest as the [*ekstatikon*] pure and simple.
Temporality is the primordial 'outside-of-itself' in and for itself."[8] Apparently, then, our time experience has a threefold structure: *temporality* as projection toward the future, *historicity* as recollection of
the past, and *within-timeness* as attention to the present.[9]

Yet if Dasein is characterized ontologically by its temporal projection toward the future as possibility, it is evident that Dasein is
never a whole. In other words, because futurity ("being-ahead-of-it-
self") is constitutive for Dasein, it follows that existence must always
be out-standing, never reaching its end. If Dasein were ever to become a whole—to reach its end—no more possibilities would be open
to it, and it would thus cease to exist. For Dasein, then, to be a whole
means to be *toward* one's end, but never to be *at* one's end. This phenomenon Heidegger calls "Being-toward-Death."

Indeed, if existence is a thrown-project, and if projection means
being-toward-possibilities, then we could say that "with death Dasein stands before its ownmost potentiality-for-Being . . . a possibility
in which the issue is nothing less than Dasein's Being-in-the-world."[10]
In Being-toward-Death Dasein comes face to face with its very being-
in-the-world as such and therefore with its own temporal foundation.
On such a view, Dasein projectively encounters the possibility of its
own impossibility, that is, its potentiality for being-a-whole. In such

---

[7]Ibid., 375-376.

[8]Ibid., 377.

[9]Ricoeur, "Human Experience," 12.

[10]Heidegger, *Being and Time,* 294.

moments, Dasein actively gathers itself up temporally, so to speak, and in so doing it grasps its own/authentic (*eigentlich*) being there in the world as a finite possibility. Authentic existence is achieved, then, in this movement of *temporal self-gathering.* "Essential authenticity ... forces the narrow *Jetzpunkt* of daily time into continuous oscillation toward the deeper horizons of an authentic futurity, by always revivifying the realization that I am *Sein-zum-Tode,* and toward the authentic past, by always viewing the now in terms of the rich possibilities presented by my tradition."[11]

"Authenticity," then, refers to Dasein's ownmost (*eigenst*) possibility for Being as temporality. Being-toward-Death reveals this possibility by disclosing Dasein's own impossibility, namely its potentiality for being-a-whole, a potentiality that Dasein may appropriate only in an act of ecstatic (temporal) self-gathering. Here, however, we are again reminded of the other direction of self-temporalization, disclosed by Dasein's unique constitution—the dimension of historicity or recollection of the past (Wiederholung). On the basis of Thomas Langan's description, quoted above, then, it must be noted that the event of self-gathering my organize itself in one of two directions. Because authenticity is a "deepening" or, if you will, an explosion of the present moment, it is necessarily a movement away from here, that is, away from *within-timeness* and the mundanity of everydayness. Accordingly, this event will direct itself either toward the future or toward the past. In any case, the self will be gathered up resolutely in anticipation or recollection. I do not mean, however, that anticipatory resolve—the event of self-gathering in Heidegger's terms—excludes an appropriative recollection of the past.[12] Nor, as I will argue, does recollective resolve—the event of mythic self-gathering—exclude an effective anticipation of a future.[13]

I would contend that in every event of self-gathering, there are elements of recollection as well as anticipation. Remember, this event

---

[11]Thomas Langan, *The Meaning of Heidegger* (New York: Columbia University Press, 1971) 54-55.

[12]See Heidegger, *Being and Time,* division 2, part 2.

[13]See below, "Recollective Resolve and the Orientation of Mythic Temporality."

is founded upon the essential temporality of human existence, and thus each movement will disclose the reality of finite being-in-the-world in its entirety, including recollection of the past, resoluteness in the present, and anxious anticipation of one's future. Because of the tendency of the present toward falling, however, any particular event of ecstatic self-gathering must derive its basic momentum from either one or the other direction of temporal movement, either the *arche* or the telos of human existence. Thus, as I shall demonstrate below, while for Heidegger Dasein is able to come *to itself* as already having been, mythic Dasein comes *from itself* and is thereby *enabled* to return to itself as one who was to be. Unfortunately, we are far ahead of ourselves at this point. Further discussion of this issue must await an analysis of temporal intuition in the myth-making experience.

IN ILLO TEMPORE, AB ORIGINE: PERIODICITY AND THE TEMPORALITY OF THE SACRED

If we are to uncover time as the ontological horizon or meaning of mythic Dasein, and if we are to proceed hermeneutically, we must first consider the concrete intuition of time in myth-making experience. As I indicated above, such an analysis must be guided from the outset by the phenomenon of mythic narrative. In the ritual narration of sacred events in illo tempore, we will discover the genuine foundation of mythic subjectivity as Wiederholung, the effective retrieve of those potentialities given with Dasein's being-in-the-world as a finite possibility. The present analysis will therefore direct itself, in part, to the temporal structure or meaning of mythic narrative.

I demonstrated earlier that temporality, like spatiality, articulates itself in terms of Dasein's original field of presence, namely, *how* Dasein experiences the intentional correlation of body-subject and world. In this regard, I found that mythic Dasein appears to be overdetermined by the phenomenon of thrownness, experiencing itself as *given over* to the world, indeterminately enveloped by its natural horizon. Indeed, mythic Dasein is so intimately engaged by its world that it understands its existence basically in terms of enabling power, the pouvoir that emerges at the interface of its compact intentional relations with the surrounding environment. Accordingly, mythic Dasein will probably be sensitive first and foremost to the biocosmic rhythms associated with its own situated being in the world. In fact, it seems only natural that the compact structure of myth-making experience gives voice, not to an intuition of time that is rectilinear, irreversible, and abstract, but rather to one that is concrete, periodic, and thus capable of repetition.

Maurice Leenhardt offers a few illustrations of this temporal periodicity in its more predominantly cosmological-ecological dimensions.

> The Australian aborigines make their cultivation season begin with the appearance of the Pleiades. The Kiwi of New Guinea date all their months from the successive disappearance over the horizon of various stars, some of which are scarcely known to the layman. They also find in the *rocking motions* of the constellations signs of times for [significant cultural] activities. ... The Canaque [as well] is an outstanding observer of nature, and he is [especially] sensitive to the *feeling of its rhythms in himself.*[14]

This point was quite evident, as well, in the passage I quoted earlier from Frazer's *Belief in Immortality.* As Frazer indicated, the natives of San Juan Capistrano would gather together at the appearance of the new moon and sing, "As the old moon dieth and cometh to life again, so we also having to die will live again."

The initiation rites of passage among the Australian aborigines, discussed earlier, are also representative of a truly dynamic existential periodicity in terms of which mythic Dasein first discovers the various modes of its own temporal being and becoming. Indeed, within the cult proper, initiation takes the form of an explicit return to the Dreamtime in order to reclaim and repeat those creative founding events ab origine. Thus like the periodicities of nature herself (lunar, solar, or ecological), the initiation rites enact the passage from the old to the new by way of a return to the beginning.

In myth-making experience the intuition of temporal movement is therefore initially related to the natural and cosmic periodicities that are, after all, only the intentional horizon of correlative rhythms in man's own biosocial existence. Such periodicity may be observed, for example, in the structure of mythic narration.

Before we examine the uniqueness of myth, however, let us be certain that myth acts, in part, like other narrative events. Like all narratives, historical or fictional, myth functions to locate man within

---

[14]Leenhardt, *Do Kamo,* 77, 83.

time, that is, at the level of an everyday existence. In a mythic plot, for example, we discover heroic deeds taking place within time. The mythic hero must always contend with or reckon with chronological duration. Even in this respect, however, the narrative succeeds in disclosing the concrete character of our dealings in time and not merely some representation of time as an abstract linear progression.[15]

On the other hand, unlike historical narrative, oral mythic narration typically demonstrates an underlying movement of repetition and return. Stylistically, we find this movement represented by repeated refrains, choruses, or phrases in the story. We read, for example, from *The Canaanite Poem of Baal,* a comprehensive seasonal myth from the ancient Near East:

> *[At length,] in the seventh year,*
> *the godling Mot is roused from his fall,*
> *and (thus) addresses Baal:*
> *"'Twas through thee, O Baal,*
> *I experienced disgrace;*
> *'twas through thee I experienced*
> *being scattered in a sieve;*
> *'twas through thee I experienced*
> *being ripped up with a sword;*
> *'twas through thee I experienced*
> *being burned in fire;*
> *'twas through thee [I experienced]*
> *[being gr]ound in a mill;*
> *'twas through (thee) I experi[enced]*
>   * * * * *
> *'twas through thee I experienced*
> *that my remains were strewn o'er the fields;*
> *'twas through thee I experienced*
> *that my morsels were cast upon the sea!"*[16]

Such formal stylistic repetition suggests that myth is concerned primarily, not with chronological duration, but with periodicity and return. Indeed, through the repeated refrains of the story, mythic Dasein begins to confront the essential periodicity of its own temporal being and becoming.

---

[15]Ricoeur, "Human Experience," 25-26.

[16]Theodore Gaster, *Thespis* (New York: Norton, 1977) 225.

We can see this concern for periodicity and repetition in the temporal form of myth's narrative structure as well. While historical narrative emphasizes an episodic (*historisch*) flow of events from past to future, myth is decidedly retrospective. The mythic plot bends over backward, recalling the story (*Geschichte*) of Dasein's origin—that time when his fate (*Geschick*) was sealed—demonstrating the periodicity of temporal experience. Let us consider a few exemplary passages. *Enuma elish* opens with the following verse:

> *When on high the heaven had not been named,*
> *Firm ground below had not been called by name,*
> *Naught but primordial Apsu, their begetter,*
> *(And) Mummu-Tiamat, she who bore them all,*
> *Their waters commingling as a single body;*
> *No reed hut had been matted, no marsh land had appeared,*
> *When no gods whatever had been brought into being,*
> *Uncalled by name, their destinies undetermined—*
> *Then it was that the gods were formed within them.*[17]

Then again, in Genesis we read,

> *In the beginning God created the heavens and the earth.*
> *The earth was without form and void*
> *and darkness was upon the face of the deep;*
> *and the Spirit of God was moving over the face of the waters.*[18]

Once more, in the Gospel of John we find:

> *In the beginning was the Word,*
> *and the Word was with God,*
> *and the Word was God.*
> *He was in the beginning with God;*
> *and all things were made through him,*
> *and without him was not anything made that was made.*[19]

This recollection of origins suggests that mythic narrative is directed primarily to retrieving the power of Dasein's finite ground. Through repetition of the story, the myth maker recognizes that his present

---

[17]Isaac Mendelsohn, ed., *Religions of the Ancient Near East* (New York: Liberal Arts Press, 1955) 19.

[18]*The New Oxford Annotated Bible,* RSV, Genesis 1:1-2.

[19]Ibid., John 1:1-3.

everyday existence, as well as any anticipated future, depends essentially upon his fateful foundational past. Thus while myth does not ignore the episodic dimension of being-within-time, characterized by a chronological flow of events from past to future, it is more concerned with a reversal of that representation, reflecting the essential periodicity of "lived-time" and the creative power at the foundation of human finitude.

Now, this inchoate apprehension of lived-time, as with man's early intuition of space, is founded upon Dasein's existence as a thrown-project, generating itself out of that intentional engagement between body-subject and world. For the Melanesian, for example, the moon's significance lies in its rhythmic waxing and waning, because in that very motion are indicated "the periods of farming, fishing, hunting and building" and therefore, the very flow and periodicity of human life iself.[20] The same type of claim may be advanced for the intuition of time in any number of diverse cultures and geographical locations. In Africa, for example, the Kaguru, Tiv, Nuer, and Lugbara all maintain a yearly ritual cycle, according to which times are fixed in terms of "man's relationship with nature, that is[,] to the ecological cycle of the year and its rhythm."[21] Thus cosmic and natural phenomena gain significance for human life only insofar as the periods marked by their rhythmic passage are experienced as crucial to the temporal ordering of affairs-in-the-body-in-the-world.

In this view, time is less a quantitative measure than a qualitative event, For it is linked fundamentally to the various exigencies and concerns associated with the transcendence of human embodment and the experience of power to which it gives rise. As I noted earlier,

---

[20]Leenhardt, *Do Kamo,* 76.

[21]John Parratt, "Time in Traditional African Thought," *Religion* 7 (Autumn 1977): 117. See also G. Barden, "Reflections of Time," *Human Context* 5 (Summer 1973): 331-43; Evans-Pritchard, *The Nuer* (Oxford: Clarendon Press, 1940) chap. 3; C. Geertz, "Person, Time, and Conduct in Bali," *The Interpretation of Cultures* (New York: Basic Books, 1973) 360-411; A. Hallowell, "Temporal Orientation in Western Civilization and in a Preliterate Society," *American Anthropologist* 39 (1937): 647-70; E. Leach, "Two Essays Concerning the Symbolic Representation of Time," in *Rethinking Anthropology* (London: Athlone Press, 1961) 124-36; D. Tait, *The Konkomba of Northern Ghana* (London: Oxford University Press, 1961) chap. 2.

because of the intimate connection between power and the sacred in human experience, it is easy to see why the mythical recognition of any critical phases in life has a specifically religious quality or significance. In fact, there is a deep sense of sacrality adhering to all mythic-ritual observances of natural and biosocial rhythms.[22]

In light of this primeval intuition of being and becoming, and its implicit connection with the sacred, there is understandably an aura of prestige for the origins in myth and ritual observance. Indeed, if periodicity is the underlying mode of temporal experience (that is, if the myth maker's life-world is grasped according to the beginning and ending of various biosocial-cosmic cycles), then it will be in the very nature of this experience to venerate the living past: the most crucial, powerful, and thus sacred moments are those of the origin (and end) of different cycles. Beginning and end are the creative and critical moments in life par excellence, as is attested by Heidegger's own existential consideration of the phenomenon of "Being-toward-Death." Each beginning is the origin of a particular mode of being, that is, a new social status, cultural norm, political institution, or public work or even the present state of the cosmos. By the same token, the end of a cycle signals not only the conclusion or termination of a previous mode of being. It also heralds (indeed it effects) the movement into a new period or mode of being. It is in short a new beginning, disclosing new possibilities of existence.

For this reason myths are concerned with origins, and primitive cosmogonies, with a beginning before all time. Even in the myths of historical cultures, namely those sacred stories whose heroes are real historical agents, we invariably find the historical acts of those heroes treated as primal, world-founding events with a truly mythical status, that is, events that usher in a new beginning, a new heaven and a new earth, the kingdom of God, or a new aeon. In so doing, these primal events bring an end to the old order, the aeon of evil or darkness.

James G. Hart has offered some important remarks on this dimension of mythic time and periodicity. Comparing myth with the phenomenon of nostalgia, Hart notes that, like the latter, mythic tem-

---

[22]Leenhardt, *Do Kamo,* 79.

porality is aeonic. The mythic hero "has a mode of being wherein [his] present is not fleeting."[23]

> True, there is often an 'elapse' of time in mythic accounts [that is, the everyday flow of within-timeness]. A hero, e.g., Hermes, is born; the years pass, he grows—all of these events happen within passing time (Kronos). But the child is not long out of his cradle before heroic deeds begin to be performed [or heroic events begin to befall him]. That is, he grows up almost immediately and reaches the eternal age proper to him.[24]

Such an understanding of temporal being is certainly evident in the sacred narratives that comprise the New Testament accounts of the birth, ministry, and death of Jesus of Nazareth. In the Gospel of Matthew, for example, after the genealogy of the first chapter, the redactor simply opens with the following statement: "Now when Jesus was born in Bethlehem of Judea in the days of Herod the king, wise men from the East came to Jerusalem saying, 'where is he who has been born king of the Jews? For we have seen his star in the East, and have come to worship him.'"[25]

Mark 1:9-11 narrates Jesus' first public appearance: "*In those days* Jesus came from Nazareth of Galilee and was baptized by John in the Jordan. And when he came up out of the water, immediately he saw the heavens opened and the Spirit descending upon him like a dove; and a voice came from heaven, 'thou are my beloved Son; with thee I am well pleased'." Thus as the Gospel accounts testify, Jesus was not out of the cradle, nor even born for that matter,[26] before his heroic or aeonic stature is made manifest—both to those within the story and to the hearers of the sacred narrative. As the quotation from Mark makes clear, even before his ministry actually begins, his first public appearance at baptism is attended by marvelous signs testifying to his divine-heroic nature and his special "aeonic" mission. This mythic-aeonic mission is summed up with the saying in Mark 1:15.

---

[23]James G. Hart, "Towards a Phenomenology of Nostalgia," *Man and World* 6 (November 1973): 415.

[24]Ibid., 413.

[25]*The New Oxford Annotated Bible*, RSV, Matt. 2:1-2.

[26]See Luke 1:1-2:21.

"The time is fulfilled, the kingdom of God is at hand; repent and believe in the Gospel."

Actually, the Gospel of Mark is basically a narrative re-presentation of this central theme by means of "gathering together" the episodic events of Jesus' ministry into one coherent structure (plot) that may ritually be repeated in the life of each and every believer. I agree, then, with Hart when he writes, "Mythic aeonic time is a mode of being which founds an epoch or aeon which perdures as a melody perdures. Within this temporal mode of being there is novelty and change, but the past is never irretrievably lost and always immanently present in the actual present."[27] In this respect, the mythic narration allows for a genuine retrieval of possibilities opened up by those archetypal events of a remembered (inherited) past, events that continue to exercise control over the myth maker's present-becoming-future.

Here again we come face to face with the periodicity of mythic time. This intuition of the sacred past as periodically recoverable within the living present will become absolutely crucial in further consideration of the constitution of mythic subjectivity. In the meantime I simply note that for myth-making Dasein the present state of affairs is fundamentally related to actions or events executed by divine personages and/or heroic ancestors, in illo tempore, ab origine. Furthermore, the present epoch remains vital only because the power of those events (ab origine) is effectively re-presented through oral recitation of the narrative within the actual situation of the believer.

Moreover, in mythic narrative—where repetition appears to be constitutive of the temporal form itself—the plot seemingly recalls the archetypal pattern or meaning of the heroic events. This pattern, summarized in an idea or theme (for example, "The kingdom of God is at hand, repent and believe in the Gospel"), enables the myth maker to repeat that sacred past within his everyday present. The mythic plot thus provides a "transition" from the episodic flow of events to the event of temporal return (Wiederholung) and existential self-renewal.[28]

---

[27]Hart, "Towards a Phenomenology," 415-16.

[28]On this point I am grateful for Ricoeur's discussion, in "Human Experience," 31, 26.

As I demonstrated, such is the case even if that "time of the beginning" can be reckoned by historical memory, for example, in the
Exodus story of the Old Testament or in the narration of the death
and resurrection of Jesus of Nazareth in the New Testament. "For example, the Passover ritual in Judaism reenacts a highly important
event that once occurred to the children of Israel; their delivery from
bondage in Egypt [and the beginning of a new life and era]." So too
with the story of Jesus' life, ministry, and death; wherever it is re-
counted in the baptismal or eucharistic celebrations of the Church,
"the historical event functions as myth."[29] In either case, Jewish or
Christian, the narration betrays the mythic-aeonic character of the
biblical events. That is, the biblical events found a new epoch or aeon;
and these foundational events, although past, are never lost but always vitally present within the concrete situation of the hearer.

We see, then, that in myth the present moment is qualified by a
special sacred temporality, through identification with originary
events of a primordial, archetypal past. The mythical nomination of
an event in illo tempore, ab origine, signifies, in effect, the *powerfulness* (and thus the sacrality) that the phenomenon has exercised and
continues to exercise over the myth maker's present situation. Upon
the founding archetypal events of that time rests the efficacy, sacrality, and significance of the myth maker's reality.

In myth-making experience, every culturally significant activity
or life-crisis situation (indeed, every *intentional* relation with one's
milieu) finds its exemplary model, its archetype, in this sacred time
of the Beginning. The present is not a product of mundane causes oc-
curring in a recent or even distant historical past. Rather it is effectively related only to those primordial events that transpired in that
originary, "aeonic" time in illo tempore. This is the hallmark of the
mythic intuition of time.

Apparently, then, myth-making Dasein simply disregards the recent historical (*historisch*) past as effectively related to the present
that he is concerned to address. Mythic narrative represents not historical events but events that are archetypal, originary, and paradig-

----

[29]Ninian Smart, "Cross-Religious Comparisons," in W. Capps, ed., *Ways
of Understanding Religion* (New York: Macmillan, 1972) 210 (both quota-
tions).

matic in the fullest sense of that word: they are events of a sacred (aeonic) time of the origin that ground and empower the present reality.

The situation is slightly different, however, in the case of biblical narrative. Here the mythical and the historical become fused: there is a "historicization" of myth and a "mythicization" of history such that the mythic power of the origin is *miraculously* located within real events of an historical time and space. As Ivan Engnell has argued in reference to Old Testament *Heilsgeschichte,* the motifs of the Sacred History, "of Exodus and Conquest and of the Convenant renewal of the cultic community grew out of a progressive historicizing of mythological forms."[30] In other words, the mighty deeds of Yahweh, the subject and substance of the Israelite cult, were not simply the atemporal acts of some divinity in a mythic past. Rather they are part and parcel of the historical memory of national ancestors acting and being acted upon in a distant but not ahistorical past. In the New Testament as well, while the narrative events of Christ's birth, death, and resurrection are certainly of a mythical status, (namely, originary events of a world destroying-world founding nature, aeonic and eminently repeatable in the life of the believer by various means of mythic identification), they nevertheless also refer to the real historical events of the life and death of the historical figure, Jesus of Nazareth.

In any event, while myth (or sacred history) is living testimony to these originary events, the myth maker or believer effectively retrieves the sacred past by means of ritual, reenacting the powerful events of That Time within the context of a living present. Through narrative means of repetition and return, present and sacred past are made to coincide, with the net result that one's concrete situation is *empowered* and sacralized. Repeating the mythical event, ritual reconstitutes the efficacy of the Origin. Here the mere flow of mundane time is arrested and profane history suspended. Indeed, we might say that the mythic-ritual gestures *collapse* history and historical distance[31] so that the actors participate in that time before time, restoring its productivity and revitalizing the present cosmos.

---

[30]F. M. Cross, *Canaanite Myth and Hebrew Epic* (Cambridge MA: Harvard University Press, 1973) 81.

[31]See A. Sadler, "Myth as Collapsed History," *Horizon* 3 (1976): 221-42.

The myth-making experience of time continuously moves in this
pendulary fashion between present and Origin. Every new activity or
institution, each new settlement or sanctuary, is realized (established) and situated by a process of mythico-ritual identification.
Speaking of this process in ancient Egypt, for example, John Wilson
reminds us that "it is not unusual [for] an important shrine, like that
at the new capital of Memphis, [to] claim participation in the creation
myth."[32] Indeed, while the primeval hill of creation was traditionally
located at Heliopolis, the home of the creator sun-god *Ra,* it was possible as well for "each Holy of Holies throughout the land [to] be
identified with the primeval hill. ... For when a new temple was
founded, it was assumed that the potential *sacredness* of the site became manifest."[33] Wilson thus concludes that "every important shrine
in Egypt seems to have had its creation mound, recognized as the
Place of the Creation," ab origine.[34]

It appears finally that the predominant apprehension of time in
mythic existence is an oscillatory motion between origin and present.
In effect, this becomes an experience of the periodic reclamation of
the sacred, a continual reliving of the power and efficacy that grounds
the present cosmos. Interpreted ontologically, in other words, mythic
Dasein constantly recognizes the present moment of existence as well
as its possibilities for being toward the future as *empowered* by a fundamentally constitutive past. The man of myth, the religious man, lives
therefore not simply within mundane chronological time but, more
important, *out of* a present moment (*Augenblick*) that undergoes
constant renewal through a "gathering up" or "gathering together" of
the past—a mythic identification with those sacred, founding events
of tradition—in the narrative event of living toward the future.

Thus myth and ritual are not means of denying, fleeing from, or
overcoming the reality of human historicity but rather affirm the underlying finitude of existence as well as its ambiguous, awe-inspiring,
or sacred ground. Ritual is, in this respect, an event of world foun-

<hr />

[32]John Wilson, *The Culture of Ancient Egypt* (Chicago: University of Chicago Press, 1965) 58.

[33]Frankfort, et al., *Before Philosophy,* 30-31.

[34]Wilson, *Ancient Egypt,* 58.

dation and self-renewal. Its concern is to maintain a living and situated involvement in the power that undergirds the actual conditions of life. Myth's concern with origins is thus not pseudo-ateological. Myth does not seek, in other words, to be either a scientific or a historical explanation of objectively causal origins. Rather it is the vital gesture of a truly ontological concern, indeed, a religious concern for the awe-inspiring and originary ground (Power) upon which life in the real world actually depends.

REPETITION, RETRIEVE, AND THE PROBLEM OF MYTHIC SUBJECTIVITY

I have suggested, following Heidegger, that time is the horizon of the meaning of mythic Dasein. When we directed our attention to the expression of temporal intuition in mythic narrative, we noticed that mythic existence temporalizes itself in a unique mode of cyclical periodicity, oscillation, or return. We now confront the following question. If periodicity or cyclical return is the ontological ground of the meaning of mythic Dasein, then what is the constitution of that being (or subjectivity) articulated in and through this temporality of repetition? Otherwise stated: if mythic existence constitutes meaning through the ritual repetition of sacred events in illo tempore, ab origine, what is the content of that meaning? What self-understanding is disclosed in and through such experience? If we can respond to this query, we will have gone a good distance toward answering the questions posed at the beginning of part 2 regarding the "who" of mythic Dasein and the constitution of mythic subjectivity.

We have seen that mythic Dasein narrates temporal movement basically in the form of a nonlinear, dynamic periodicity. Mythic existence is characterized, so to speak, by this cyclical or pendulary movement between a sacred past and the present. Indeed, as Edmund Leach has suggested, it might be more correct to call this a pendulary rather than a cyclical experience of temporal change simply because the notion of movement in a circle is perhaps too abstract a description of the repetitive oscillation between archetypal past and present.[35] Furthermore, by considering mythic time in terms of a pendulary movement, we are more likely to recognize the simi-

---

[35]Leach, "Two Essays," chap. 6.

larity between this experience of time and Heidegger's existential discussion of temporal retrieve, or Wiederholung. Mythic existence is, in its very essence, a movement of repetition, a return to the sacred time of the origins and a retrieval of the power of those sacred events in the local here and now of the believer.

Now, it has been argued by some philosophers and historians of religion that such a pendulary movement of return is a nostalgic longing for paradise lost, an expression of the myth maker's fear of temporal process, an attempt to flee from the finitude of his own historicity, to annul the flow of meaningless duration and live in the ahistorical, supernaturally eternal Now.[36] I contend, however, that such an interpretation of sacred time and temporal return in mythic existence betrays a naive view of the phenomenon under consideration. I will demonstrate, to the contrary, that by means of this periodic narrative repetition of the origins (for example, the events attributed to the Dreamtime or to some other sacred past), mythic Dasein is put in touch with pure historicity in a most fundamental way. Indeed, in the mythic temporality of repetition we will discover an authentic temporalizing of finite temporality.

In the narrative event of returning to and recollecting its origins, mythic Dasein implicitly recognizes the finitude of its existence, namely, its finite possibilities as well as the factical situatedness of its embodiment. "In that time," "At the beginning," "In those days," "Once upon a time"—all such formulas indicate the event of mythic repetition. Such movement suggests that one's horizons do not open out infinitely upon any conceivable range of actions or events, that all present choices as well as future possibilities are limited by that which has gone before. All actions are constrained by the "having been" of one's sacred tradition, bounded by the "facticity" of Dasein's primordial thrownness. In the act of return and repetition the future of one's present is recognized as bound up intimately with the retrieval of one's past. As Levi-Strauss has suggested, in mythic repetition, as in our periodic religious pilgrimages to sacred places or venerated objects, "the *contradiction* of a completed past and a

---

[36]See especially Eliade, *Cosmos and History.*

present in which it survives [is] surmounted."[37] In surmounting this contradiction, or in overcoming this *ecstatical tension,* a vital reappropriation (*Eignung*) of one's primordial coming-to-be in the world is effected. Indeed, this is the case in all archaic New Year celebrations of cosmic renewal. One's creative (foundational) past is gathered up productively into one's present-becoming-future, a process that I have called an authentic temporalizing of finite temporality and to which I referred earlier when I spoke of the ecstatic self-gathering of mythic Dasein in the movement of recollective resolve.[38]

Now, on this view, the future is not an open region of pure possibility before which one is set free to exercise uninhibited movement toward an ever-receding horizon of infinite progress. Rather in such an event of *recollective* self-gathering, the future is felt (*erlebt*) as a finite set of meaningful possibilities made actual only on the ground of an enabling past (or tradition) that is periodically "gathered up" (*aufgehoben*) within the present moment of decision (*Augenblick*). Tradition is thereby carried forward, as we indicate when we speak of appropriating (*aneignen*) one's factical existence in the present-of-living-toward-one's future. All three ecstasies are thus integrated within the event of mythic Dasein's unique mode of temporal becoming as repetition or recollective resolve.

To elucidate further the meaning of mythic subjectivity in terms of this temporality of repetition or recollective resolve, I must discuss in greater detail the temporal mode characteristic of the phenomenon of being thrown, that is, the mode of the "having been." The justification for such a discussion lies in our earlier discovery that mythic Dasein is primordially determined by thrownness or its having to be. That is, mythic existence articulates itself principally in response to the experience of power—the experience of being rooted within and "delivered up to the world in such a way that it is overwhelmed by that to which it is delivered up."[39]

---

[37]Claude Lévi-Strauss, "Time Regained," in *The Savage Mind* (Chicago: University of Chicago Press, 1966) 242.

[38]See, e.g., Heidegger, *Being and Time,* 437f.

[39]Martin Heidegger, *The Piety of Thinking,* ed. J. Hart (Bloomington: Indiana University Press, 1976) 43.

In the first section of this chapter I noted that the ontological horizon or meaning of thrownness (facticity) is to be sought in the temporal mode of the "having been." *"Bringing Dasein face to face* with the 'that-it-is' of its own thrownness ... becomes existentially possible only if Dasein's Being ... constantly *is* as having been."[40] That is, Dasein discovers itself as thrown insofar as it has a past whence it comes. If Dasein did not exist as "having been," then the phenomenon of "being in the throw" would make no sense whatsoever.

As "having been," Dasein is given over to a world, determined *in advance* by that situation in which it finds itself already predisposed (*Befindlichkeit.*) Accordingly, " 'being-thrown' means finding oneself in some state-of-mind or other."[41] Our mood or predis-position, then, discloses existence in terms of facticity, namely, *how* we find ourselves already oriented within the world. State of mind, or mood, reveals that we are grounded in the past and that we exist always as having been. Still, if mood serves to disclose how we are as having been, then it would follow that our mood is the means through which we may exist in a movement of return, *bringing us back* to the facticity of our own situated being *there* in the world. In fact, as Heidegger suggests, "the thesis that 'one's state-of-mind is grounded primarily in having-been' means that the existentially basic character of mood lies in *bringing* one *back* to something."[42]

Several questions force themselves upon us at this point. To what are we brought back in this disclosure of the having been? What does it mean to say that we are brought back to something? How is this "bringing back" achieved? I would suggest, at first, that we should interpret the expression "to be brought back" (*zurückbringen*) as referring to an event of ecstatic self-gathering. The phrase indicates that movement whereby Dasein is *gathered up* or collected into itself, and its temporally strewn-out existence is brought together in a decisive moment. In other words, Dasein is recalled from its usual mode of being dispersed among things within the world. Evidently, then, we are brought back to our own being or ground. The character of that

---

[40]Heidegger, *Being and Time,* 390.

[41]Ibid., 389.

[42]Ibid., 390.

being to which we are brought back, however, depends upon several factors. In large measure, it depends on the content of that mood by means of which the movement of self-gathering occurs. As Heidegger suggests, the state of mind that prevails when Dasein is overdetermined by the experience of its own facticity or thrownness (as is mythic Dasein) is that of anxiety.

> Anxiety brings Dasein face to face with its ownmost Being-thrown. . . . That-in-the-face-of which one has anxiety is indeed already 'there'— namely, Dasein itself. . . . [Anxiety thus] brings one back to the pure "that-it-is" of one's ownmost individualized thrownness . . . back to one's thrownness as something *possible* which *can be repeated.*[43]

Thrown into the world, Dasein exists on the basis of its having been. "Having been" means that Dasein finds itself in one mood or another. Mood, therefore, has the capacity to bring Dasein back to the facticity of its own existence. In the mood of anxiety, Dasein is brought all the way back to the nakedness of its ownmost being thrown into the world as finite possibility. As Heidegger's comments here indicate, repetition is the *how* of that event of ecstatic self-gathering whereby in anxiety Dasein comes back to its thrown being in the world as such. Brought face to face with its uncanny being-there as a thrown possibility, Dasein thus *comes back to itself,* collects itself, so to speak, and "takes over resolutely that entity which it already is."[44] Through the movement of repetition, then, finite, factical existence succeeds in temporalizing itself authentically. Herein lies the meaning of "being brought back." Through that movement of ecstatic self-gathering, finite existence resolutely turns back to itself and faces its own finitude. This event of authentic existence, according to Heidegger, is properly designated by the term "anticipatory resolve."

Now, Calvin Schrag has claimed that Heidegger's notion of "repetition" (*Wiederholung*) as it relates to the event of authenticity should not be confused with some sort of primitive "doctrine of the eternal recurrence of the same within an unending cosmic cycle." As he contends, repetition is "neither a recurrence in the sense of a reenactment of that which previously happened, nor does it have to

---

[43]Ibid., 393-94.
[44]Ibid., 388.

do with factual incidents or datable events."[45] Heidegger agrees in part when he states, "Arising, as it does, from a resolute projection of one-self, repetition does not let itself be persuaded of something by what is 'past', just in order that this, as something which was formerly ac-tual, may recur."[46] Thus while Schrag may be correct in denying that repetition has to do with the re-presentation of actual past events, he has not convinced this author at least that *Wiederholung,* or retrieve, is necessarily contrary to the temporality of repetition at the basis of the mythic experience of power and the recovery of sacred events in illo tempore. Indeed, contrary to Schrag, Thomas Sheehan has even suggested that

> in that dimension of retrieve called historicity Heidegger speaks of a *Sichüberliefern der Möglichkeiten'* (SZ 383f.), which is not the 'hand-ling down' of possibilities as the existing English translation has it, but a 'freeing up' of possibilities for oneself, a destruction-retrieve *formally homologous* with the classical therapeutic process deline-ated by Freud and *with the reactualization of archetypes in primitive cultures.*[47]

We need to consider this point in greater detail. I have suggested at various times throughout my discussion that the movement of mythic repetition and recollective retrieve is an event of authenticity not unlike the authenticity of anticipatory resolve described by Hei-degger. Using the above recommendation by Sheehan as a direct charge, I will now explicitly examine the relationship between these two modes of being to articulate more specifically the constitution or meaning of mythic subjectivity. I will begin by displaying some of the more salient resemblances between these two events of Wied-erholung, repetition or retrieve.

We saw above that mythic Dasein experiences itself primarily in terms of facticity, that is, in terms of throwness. This characteristic is especially evident in its concrete absorption in the world, over-determined by that situation wherein it finds itself having to be. Ac-

---

[45]Calvin Schrag, "Heidegger on Repetition and Historical Understand-ing," *Philosophy East and West* 20 (1970): 289.

[46]Heidegger, *Being and Time,* 438.

[47]T. Sheehan, "Getting to the Topic: The New Edition of *Wegmarken,"Re-search in Phenomenology* 7 (1977): 312.

cordingly, it would appear that the state of mind characteristic of mythic Dasein is one of anxiety. As Heidegger indicated above, in anxiety Dasein genuinely finds itself facing its thrown being in the world. I would recommend, however, that we designate this mythic mood of anxiety by use of the term "awe." Indeed, I contend generally that anxiety is a state of mind more characteristic of Dasein when it anticipates the looming presence of what is "ahead of one"—facticity as disclosed futurally (end). Awe on the other hand is the state of mind that seems to predominate when Dasein finds itself overwhelmed by the weighty presence of the given or "what has been given"—facticity as disclosed in its "having been" (*arche*). In any case, mythic Dasein, anxious or in awe about its being-there, is overwhelmed by the uncanniness of its facticity—it "having to be."

In this mood of awe, thrown back upon its finite presence in the world, mythic existence is gathered up and temporalizes itself in the ecstatic mode of repetition—"going back into the possibilities of the Dasein [its mythic hero] that has-been-there."[48] Repetition here means a recollective reappropriation of Dasein's own powerful ground in the guise of mythic-heroic deeds. This repetition is made possible through the plot structure of the mythic narration. In narrative identification with, and ritual repetition of, heroic acts in illo tempore, ab origine, mythic Dasein finds itself empowered to exist authentically in an event of ecstatic self-gathering. Indeed, as Heidegger himself suggests, the concrete expression of genuine resolve or authentic existence is to be found in the ontic repetition of the possibilities that have come down to one through one's tradition.

In view of this analysis, I would suggest that that in the mythic temporality of repetition and its movement of recollective retrieve there is disclosed an event of authentic temporalizing of finite temporality that is not unlike the event of authenticity described by Heidegger in his analysis of anticipatory resolve. For Heidegger, authentic Dasein exists futurally in the advent (*Zukunft, avenir*) of itself as a finite potentiality or ability to be. Mythic Dasein, on the other hand, exists in the awe-filled event of identifying itself with the *arche,* enabled or empowered to come-out-of-itself-into-its-own as the sacred

---

[48]Heidegger, *Being and Time,* 437.

hero. There are thus significant differences between these two kinds of authenticity that cannot be ignored—differences, I might add, that blinded Heidegger to the discovery of a more primordial form of authentic selfhood disclosed by myth.

The distinction is basically twofold: mythic authenticity, or recollective resolve, is primarily concerned with recovering itself as *arche* or "coming-to-be," while Heidegger's authentic Dasein is oriented toward the future as death or "coming-to-an-end." In this regard, we must also address the distinction between the past as *archetype* in mythic repetition and the past as finite possibilities of an historical tradition in anticipatory resolve. On the other hand, Heidegger's conception of authenticity involves Dasein's coming back to itself out of the world, while mythic authenticity involves coming back to oneself through identification with the mythic hero as a manifestation of power. I turn at this point to consider the first distinction, that between orientation toward the past versus orientation toward the future, and correlatively the difference between past as archetype and past as finite possibilities.

RECOLLECTIVE RESOLVE
AND THE ORIENTATION OF MYTHIC TEMPORALITY

At this point we should recall the earlier discussion concerning the distinction between anticipatory and recollective resolve, the two different ways in which the event of authenticity or ecstatic self-gathering might occur.

Remember that authenticity is the realization of one's potentiality for being-a-whole by coming to grips with the possibility of one's own impossibility, that is, by actively appropriating the consequences of one's finitude. In this event, Dasein's actual involvements within the world are partially suspended in order that the grip of mundane time may be relaxed, allowing one's present to be taken up (aufgehoben) in a movement of ecstatic self-gathering, a movement directed away from the forgetfulness of the present—either as being-toward-the-end (telos) or (as I would contend) toward-the-beginning (*arche*). Indeed, Heidegger correctly realized that one's ownmost possibility—the possibility in which one's very being-in-the-world-as-such is at stake—is disclosed in the anxious anticipation of the advent of death. Dasein does in fact come face to face with its own ecstatic-finite selfhood in the phenomenon of Being-toward-Death or being-toward-one's-end. This event Heidegger designated by the expression "anticipatory resoluteness."

Now, as Heidegger fully realized, anticipatory resolve is truly a movement of ecstatic self-gathering, including the retrieval of one's past as well as (of course) the anticipation of one's future. For Heidegger, Dasein (as thrown) is able to come back to itself as having to come to its end (the future). As Heidegger puts it,

> only in so far as Dasein *is* as an "I-*am*-as-having-been," can Dasein come towards itself futurally in such a way that it comes back. As authentically futural, Dasein *is* authentically as *"having-been."* Anticipation of one's uttermost and ownmost possibility is coming back understandingly to one's ownmost "been." Only so far as it is futural can Dasein *be* authentically as having been. The character of "having been" arises, in a certain way, from the future.[49]

I argue, however, Heidegger's position notwithstanding, that the character of the "ahead-of-itself" arises, in a certain way, from the past. Only because Dasein exists as having-been is anything like a future possible for it. Indeed, because Dasein is a thrown-project, it would make no sense to speak of it as futural if one did not also speak of this projection as a movement from somewhere, namely, the having been of one's past. Now, the distinctiveness of the phenomenon of recollective resolve or mythic authenticity begins to show itself in this very realization. Mythic Dasein comes *from* itself (as archetype) and is thereby *enabled* to come back to itself as one who had to be (the past).

We can see this, for example, in the various journeys that typify the plot structure of mythic narrative. Consider, for instance, the hero's geographical return to his homeland, as in Odysseus' return to Ithaca. Paul Ricoeur has noted, and correctly, I believe, that this return to hearth and home is, like escaping from a labyrinth in which one has been lost, a rediscovery of the self. Such a return to the origin suggests a genuine recovery of what had previously been forgotten in life's travails—one's true ground or source.

Alternatively, consider the hero's quest for immortality and eternal life. He travels far and wide only to arrive eventually at the land

---

[49]Ibid., 373.

of his ancient forefather, for example, Gilgamesh's journey to Utan-apishtim. Here as well, the journey (plot structure) leads the hero back to an origin—not to his homeland, in this case, but certainly back to his archetypal ground. Once again, the temporal and spatial movement assumes the shape of a mythic return to the self—a recovery of one's finite (but forgotten) foundation.

Finally, there is also the archetypal journey of the "first" ancestor (or firstborn of creation) back to the sacred abode of a deity or supreme creator, a journey seen as clearly in the Bagre myth of the Lo Dagaa of West Africa as in the New Testament account of Jesus' return to the right hand of God the Father. Here, too, we might recognize the journey as a narrative expression of the event of temporal self-gathering, in the mode of recollective resolve—mythically coming back to one's gound through a return to origins. The myth maker, like the hero of the story himself, returns to the origin or ground through identification with those heroic deeds in illo tempore, repeating the archetypal events ab origine.

While anticipatory resolve thus retrieves its past in the event of the advent of the future—anxiously living toward its absolute end,—recollective resolve becomes its future in the awe-filled and empowering event of returning to and retrieving its absolute beginning. In either case, the *uttermost* and *ownmost* possibility of Dasein is realized, its potentiality for nonbeing or the possibility of its never having been at all. Either way, an authentic temporalizing of finite temporality is achieved. I am suggesting in essence that the event of authentic existence is realized in a movement of ecstatic self-gathering. This movement may organize itself in one of two directions, either anxiously toward the telos (*Sein zum Tode*) or in awe toward the *arche* (*Sein zur Entstehung*) of meaningful human existence. In either case, Dasein recognizes the finitude of its being as a thrown-project, and subjectivity is thereby rescued from self-forgetfulness or lostness in the mundanity of everyday affairs. Poised basically in opposing directions—one acknowledging that Dasein has an absolute beginning, the other emphasizing its absolute end—both recollective and anticipatory resolve are seeking to articulate one and the same intuition, that being-in-the-world is finite, bounded on either side by the awe-inspiring/anxiety-producing mystery of its own possible impossibility.

It should begin to be clear to us now why the mythic event of repetition seeks to recover a past that is arche-typal, while in Heidegger's view authenticity is concerned with recovering only the finite possibilities of a historical tradition. Recollective resolve is concerned with the absolute beginning or archetypal past for the same reasons that anticipatory resolve directs itself to the uttermost future, the final end of human life. Anticipatory resolve is anxiously oriented toward the future and so is concerned with the absolute and outstanding limit of human existence (namely, death). Recollective resolve, on the other hand, is oriented toward its sacred, awe-inspiring past and so is primarily concerned with the fundamental ground of human existence, namely, its *arche,* or absolute beginning. Thus when we compare these two modes of ecstatic self-gathering, we must remember that the future of anticipation is to the past of recollection as the future of recollection is to the past of anticipation. Consequently, just as anticipatory resolve is not consciously directed toward an absolute or archetypal past but only to those finite possibilities disclosed within a particular historical tradition, so recollective resolve is concerned not with death as a final end of life but only with those new beginnings that are thereby made possible on the basis of its own sacred, archetypal past.

In this respect we should realize that recovering the possibilities provided by a sacred archetypal past is not the same as recovering those finite possibilities given within a historical tradition. The difference here is intimately related to the fact that mythic authenticity involves coming back to oneself through identification with a mythic hero, while anticipatory resolve involves coming back to oneself on one's own by coming out of the world. I will discuss this problem shortly.

In the meantime, I suggest that in myth-making experience there is a recovery of the self from its dispersion in the world of everyday and mundane affairs. Ritual identification with a mythic hero entails a moment of vision in which the self is temporarily gathered up into its own being as it is. In this moment the self recognizes its own essential finitude, repeats its awe-inspiring origins in the very event of living toward its future. We might say, in other words, that in such moments the scattered "I" of profane chronological duration (the indefinite, anonymous social self) loses its hold so that the authentic, finite, and concrete self may come to the fore.

AUTHENTIC ANONYMITY

We might seem to have reached a dilemma at this point if we tried to remain within strictly Heideggerian categories. On the one hand, we have noticed a likeness between the everyday self's becoming lost in the public domain and mythic Dasein's identification with the sacred hero. In this respect mythic existence might be interpreted, along Heideggerian lines, as an inauthentic mode of being in which the myth maker becomes determined by something other than himself. It seems that mythic identification with the hero, however, acts in a way contrary to that indicated by Heidegger's critique of everydayness. Rather, it has been demonstrated that the mythic repetition of sacred archetypes is a movement of ecstatic self-gathering, an event of authenticity not unlike that described by Heidegger in *Being and Time*. Yet here as well we have noticed that the mythic event of recollective resolve is not quite the same as anticipatory resoluteness. Accordingly, there seems to be a strange mixing of anonymity and authenticity in the mode of being of mythic Dasein.

Our dilemma can be resolved only if we turn our attention to the other major distinction between mythic subjectivity and the event of authenticity as conceived by Heidegger. That is, we must demonstrate how the event of self-gathering that is achieved by means of coming-back-to-oneself-through-the-group (in the figure of the mythic hero) differs from the event of authenticity achieved by means of coming-back-to-oneself-out-of-the-group. Moreover, we will be able to display the meaning of such difference only by considering the specificity of mythic retrieval of an archetypal past versus the authentic recovery of finite possibilities within a historical tradition.

What is mythic Dasein doing in the event of retrieving its sacred, archetypal past? How does this retrieval differ from the recovery of finite possibilities disclosed within a historical tradition? We must here recall our earlier discussion of the compact structure of mythic being-in-the-world, and the experience of power to which it gives rise. Mythic Dasein is so thoroughly enveloped within the bonds of corporeal intentionality that it experiences its engagements in the world as so many confrontations with *power*. Accordingly, this power is nothing other than a manifestation of Dasein's intentional-ecstatic foundation. In the experience of power, mythic existence thus comes face to face with its being-there-in-the-world as finite possibility.

Now, because of the tendency of embodied subjectivity to embody itself in language, this mythic experience of power will find natural expression in the narrative guise of various sacred heroes or divine ancestors in illo tempore, ab origine. The designation *in illo tempore,* however, does not refer to any particular historical past. Rather it acknowledges the ontological ground of power in temporality, and it recognizes, moreover, that the fundamental temporal mode is the having been. This "having been" is recollected in the phrase *in illo tempore,* demonstrating that, for myth, *repetition* is indeed constitutive of the temporal form of the narrative itself.[50] In mythic identification and narrative repetition of those sacred events ab origine, Dasein thus recovers the power of its own temporal foundation; it returns to itself, its being-there-in-the-world as a finite possibility. In this event it gathers up its temporally strewn-out existence, calls itself back from arbitrary dispersion in the world of mundane affairs, and, with a sense of awe, realizes its ownmost potentiality— the possibility of its never having been at all.

Recall what Bultmann suggestively argues for time and again in his demythologizing of the New Testament. In recollecting and identifying with the life of Christ, the believer effectively realizes the insecurity of his own finite being in the world and gains authentic existence in the event of recognizing his essential dependence upon a power that is both beyond him and yet within him through the mystery of grace.[51] As Bultmann's position here indicates, in the event of faith (what I would call mythic authenticity) the believer collects his existence by recovering the past as sacred-archetypal, namely, foundational for the present and the possibility of a meaningful future.

Alternatively, consider *The Epic of Gilgamesh,* a classic narration of the myth of the hero. Gilgamesh undergoes an explicit movement of self-gathering in which the various embodiments of power (for example, Huwara, the Bull of Heaven, Siduri, and so forth) ultimately bring the hero/hearer/believer face to face with the ontological insecurity that characterizes his being-in-the-world as a thrown-pro-

---

[50]Ricoeur, "Human Experience," 31.

[51]See, e.g., Rudolph Bultmann, "The New Testament and Mythology," in H. W. Bartsch, ed., *Kerygma and Myth* (New York: Harper and Row, 1961).

ject. With each trial and tribulation the hearer/hero, that is, Gilgamesh, is brought ever closer to an authentic retrieval of his own powerful, finite foundation, narratively represented by his arduous journey back to Utanapishtim. In this movement of recollective resolve, he recovers himself from an existence in which the mystery of his being-there would disappear from sight forever. In any event we find here a recognition of human finitude, a rediscovery of one's own facticity; but we also find here an acknowledgment of openness, the potentiality for change, and the realization of new possibilities that such a "being-toward-the-beginning" implies.

Let us consider at this point a more comprehensive illustration of the central claims advanced in this chapter, that the sacred hero is a manifestation of the power of embodied existence within the world; that identifying with the heroic deeds in illo tempore is an event of authenticity or mythic self-gathering in which Dasein realizes its unique (eigen) and fundamental ground.

In offering this example, I am perhaps not proposing an interpretation in the strictly literary or textual sense. In fact, if we recall our earlier claim that myth is characteristic more of oral culture than of textual-literary culture, it would follow that one cannot approach the interpretation of myth as one would interpret a written text or piece of literature. As Werner Kelber has convincingly argued in his most recent work, *The Oral and the Written Gospel,* textual hermeneutics is not adequate to the task of understanding and interpreting oral presentation.[52] We may not assume, in other words, that the meaning of a myth (as an oral/aural event), like the meaning of any literary text, is something articulable independently of the powerful mythic recitation and the event of self-transformation that it effects. Indeed, if the meaning of the myth is what it does existentially to the hearer/believer in the ritual context of mythic recollection, then no translation of the story into other, less mythic terms will be adequate to the event of understanding that it seeks to produce. To understand the myth, in other words, is not to grasp its sense in some ideal signification but to be transformed by the mythic events, to be interpreted by the myth, to understand oneself anew in view of what the

---

[52]Kelber, xv-xviii.

myth discloses. Having stated these reservations, I proceed to my illustration.

I return at this juncture to our earlier example of the Babylonian Epic of Creation, *Enuma elish*. In that myth, the various deities (Tiamat, Ea, Marduk, Apsu, and so on) were seen to be embodiments of power in the Mesopotamian's concrete engagements within his life-world, especially as these engagements were sources of *awe*, disclosing the fundamental precariousness or finitude of Dasein's being-there as a thrown-possibility. My analysis of this myth centers on three figures in particular, Marduk, Ea, and Kingu insofar as I find these three to illuminate the primordial existential function of the mythic logos.

The narrative opens with a description of the state of things before the creation of cosmos (I:1-20). Apsu and Tiamat, parents to the gods, are disturbed by the excessive clamor of their children. First Apsu, then Tiamat, seeks to destroy his offspring in an attempt to regain a condition of peace and tranquillity (I:21-50; 81-123), but they are themselves destroyed by their children as a result. Marduk, the chief protagonist or hero of the myth, the one true hope of the gods—"he whose strength is mighty"[53]—succeeds in subduing Tiamat, the primeval power of watery chaos, the waters that bring life as well as death to the Persian Gulf. The vanquishing and brutal dismemberment of Tiamat stands out as the crucial episode of the creation story. It is significant about this episode that, while the mythic event of death and dismemberment typically represents a temporal return to origins, it nevertheless stands here in the midst of a chronological movement extending through time. Thus within the narrative structure we may discover a movement of return to beginnings in order that a new world may emerge. This event of Wiederholung is, then, the existential function of the plot—Marduk's victory over Tiamat. As Ea—"master of his fathers ... broad of understanding, wise, mighty in strength, much stronger than his grandfather, Anshar"—had established his dwelling place (earth) upon the slain body of Apsu, so Marduk will create the cosmos upon the vanquished remains of Tiamat (IV). In either case, establishing their dominion over the slain carcass of primeval power, Marduk and Ea mythically reveal the self-understand-

---

[53]Heidel, *Babylonian Genesis,* 28.

ing of the ancient Mesopotamians as they seek to secure their existence upon the life-giving soil of the fertile crescent. While Ea embodies the foundational power of life-bearing earth (facticity), standing out against a horizon of watery chaos, Marduk embodies the power of possibility (futurity) and of new life, the power that the Mesopotamian experiences in his renewed attempts to exist within the world by cultivating the land against the ever-present threat of natural disaster (I:125).

Marduk's battle against Tiamat and her forces of cosmic destruction, the central event of the myth, discloses the myth maker's realization of his existence as finite facticity. Through the mythic narration, the Mesopotamian comes to grips with the experiences of power that are born of the intentional engagement of existing Dasein within the world as he recognizes his being-there as a possibility. Indeed, the centrality of this battle is reflected in the fact that the contest between Marduk and Tiamat's forces occupies four of the Tablets of the Epic, while the subsequent creation of the cosmos occupies less than two.[54] Repeating the central plot of Marduk's victory over the power of watery chaos in the establishment of a meaningful cosmos, the Mesopotamian annually[55] recalls his essential being-in-the-throw, acknowledging the mystery, ambiguity, and possible impossibility of his own existence there.

Once again, the entire scenario is mythically projected back into a primordial space and time, indicating myth's concern with the very ground of finite existence within the world. Ostensibly, the function of this return to origins is the recovery of human existence at the level of pure historicity. By returning to and re-presenting the archetypal events of that foundational past, the Mesopotamian effectively recognizes the constant tension between life and death that is the hallmark or meaning of finite being. In view of such recognition, we say that mythic Dasein comes back to itself, namely, its powerful ground as a thrown-project, in the event of repeating the heroic deeds in illo tempore. Accordingly, the event of ritual recollection is an act of authentic being-in-the-world through mythic indentification with Mar-

---

[54]Ibid., 102.

[55]Ibid., 16-17; also see Eliade, *Cosmos and History,* 55-58.

duk, the embodiment of the power of existence as it continuously rescues itself from the claws of watery chaos (Tiamat). The mythic event of ecstatic self-gathering or recollective resolve is achieved in the retrieval of this contest, where Dasein identifies itself with the sacred hero.

That the ancient Mesopotamian experienced this myth as a means of returning to the primordial ground or foundation of his existence is attested by the fact that Marduk and Ea together, victorious over Tiamat's army, fashion mankind from the blood of Kingu's slain body, the supreme leader of Tiamat's forces, the one to whom Tiamat had entrusted the tablet of destinies, the apparent representative of the established (present) regime. As the myth relates:

> *(Tiamat) exalted Kingu; in their midst she made him great.*
> *To march at the head of the army, to direct the forces,*
> *To raise the weapons for the engagement, to launch the attack,*
> *The high command of the battle,*
> *She intrusted to his hand; she caused him to sit in the assembly,*
> *(saying:)*
> *"I have cast the spell for thee, I have made thee great*
>   *in the assembly of the gods.*
> *The dominion over all the gods I have given into thy hand.*
> *Mayest thou be highly exalted, thou, my unique spouse!*
> *May thy names become greater than (those of) the*
>   *Anunnaki!"*
> *She gave him the tablet of destinies, she fastened it upon*
>   *his breast, (saying:)*
> *"As for thee, thy command shall not be changed, the word*
>   *of thy mouth shall be dependable!"*[56]

Yet it appears that Kingu's investiture was to no avail. Tiamat's forces were defeated despite his leadership. Indeed, Kingu himself was brought low before all the gods by the superior strength and strategy of Marduk.

> *As for Kingu, who had become chief among them,*
> *[Marduk] bound him and counted him among the dead gods.*
> *He took from him the tablet of destinies, which was not*
>   *his rightful possession.*
> *He sealed it with his seal and fastened it on his breast.*[57]

---

[56]Heidel, *Babylonian Genesis,* 24.

[57]Ibid., 41-42.

Kingu, given all power and authority over life and destiny, is nevertheless destroyed by Marduk, and is then mythically viewed as the
source of human existence.

> *Let him who created the strife be delivered up; . . .*
> *"Kingu it was who created the strife,*
> *And caused Tiamat to revolt and prepare for battle."*
> *They bound him and held him before Ea;*
> *Punishment they inflicted upon him by cutting (the*
>   *arteries of) his blood.*
> *With his blood they created mankind; . . .*
> *. . . . Ea, the wise, had created mankind.*[58]

This mythical nomination of Kingu (he who was invested with
power yet defeated) as the source of human existence recognizes the
fundamental ambiguity, indeed the real dilemma of finite being as
thrown into the world. In the fallen/slain figure of Kingu, the myth
maker comprehends his own fated existence within the world: powerful yet impotent—given over to the forces that dominate his present
existence there. Indeed, in the mythical triad of Kingu (impotent
power that illegitimately wears the tablet of destinies), Marduk (con-
quering, victorious power that controls destiny by offering new hope
and possibilities), and Ea (foundational creative power of earth and
human existence), mythic Dasein comes to grips with the three basic
moments of its ontological foundation (its essential finitude): Ea, the
embodiment of earthy facticity; Kingu, the embodiment of impotent
falling (present actuality); and Marduk, the embodiment of open (future) possibility.

In terms of this analysis, the ritual reenactment of the archetypal
events narrated within the Creation Epic represents an implicit return to Dasein's ownmost being, retrieving the self from its tendency
to lose itself or to take its existence in the world for granted. Mythic
Dasein thereby recognizes its fragile and hence awe-filled foundation. Repetition of the sacred past thus becomes an event of ecstatic
self-gathering, whereby the myth maker finds himself authentically
being in the world in a movement of recollective resolve. In any event,
the myth re-presents what the believing community collectively
reenacts in the *akitu,* or New Year celebration—those archetypal

---

[58]Ibid., 47.

events in illo tempore, ab origine, events that recall the power or sacrality of finite existence within the world.

I have suggested that mythic identification with the sacred hero calls Dasein back from its everyday dispersion in the world of mundane affairs, back to a more primordial absorption in its own essential being as self-temporalizing temporality. Indeed, I have argued that in the sacred temporality of repetition there is disclosed a genuine act of ecstatic self-gathering, bringing Dasein all the way back to its own finite ground, back to the *power* of is thrown-being-there-in-the-world as a possibility. In the context of ritual reenactment, mythic existence virtually gathers up or repeats its past (the creative mythic happenings in illo tempore, ab origine: its thrown ground) in the event of living *effectively* in a present-becoming-future.

Thus while anticipatory resolve calls Dasein back to its ownmost possibility in the anxious event of Being-toward-Death, the absolute end of finite being, recollective resolve calls Dasein back to itself by turning its gaze toward the other limit of human finitude—to the awe-inspiring and absolute beginning of finite existence (*Sein zur Entstehung*). We see, then, that mythic retrieval of an archetypal past is not to be compared with the recovery of finite possibilities enshrined within a historical tradition. Rather this archetypal recollection is structurally analogous to the anticipatory resolve disclosed in the phenomenon of Being-toward-Death. Both movements serve to bring Dasein back to itself, to its own (eigen) finitude—one by a movement toward the *arche,* the other by a movement toward the telos of human existence. Correlatively, the finite possibilities recovered from an historical tradition by authentic Dasein are structurally analogous to the future possibilities made available to mythic Dasein through the event of reliving one's sacred, archetypal past. For anticipatory resolve the recovery of the past as tradition is made possible only on the grounds of an *anxious* being-toward-the-future. For recollective resolve the future becomes a possibility only on the basis of *awe-filled* retrieval of the past as sacred archetype. In either case, the entire being of Dasein as a thrown-project is collected in a moment of ecstatic self-gathering.

Still, if mythic Dasein is called back to its ownmost possibility by means of identifying itself with the sacred hero, then this call must not be construed as a call of personal (individual) conscience. Rather

it should be understood as in some sense "anonymous." Indeed, it is
an ambiguous call coming from Dasein's own chiaroscuro ground,
embodied in the figure of the mythic ancestor and made accessible
through the concrete mediation of the group. In this light, the triad
of Marduk, Kingu, and Ea must be viewed as specific mythic embodiments of the ambiguous power (fungierende Intentionalität) of human existence as a thrown-project. Through oral narration of the
events in this epic, Dasein is thus called back to itself, its ownmost
potentiality for being, by means of its prepersonal foundation, realized in the event of mythic identification with the sacred hero of the
group. Thus, while mythic Dasein identifies with specific heroic
ancestors, its mode of being is called anonymous because this identification is ultimately with the prepersonal power of its own ambiguous ground.

It now appears that we find in mythic existence a unique mode of
being that Heidegger was unable to disclose by means of his analyses
in *Being and Time*. This mode of being rests upon the primordial
identity of Dasein's authentic and anonymous possibilities for being-
in-the-world. We designate this mode of being of mythic Dasein by
the term "authentic anonymity."

In order to appreciate more fully this concept of "authentic anonymity" it is necessary to draw some basic distinctions and, in this
way, to demonstrate that the present project departs significantly
from Heidegger's own analyses. The first distinction is between two
possible senses of the term "authentic," an *existentiell,* or ontic, and
an "existential," or ontological, sense. Ontically we are quite familiar
with the meaning of the English word "authentic" or the German terms
authentisch, echt, and *zuverlassig.* These may be translated as "genuine," "true," "real," "reliable," or "certain." In any event, we recognize the condition of authenticity to which these terms ordinarily
refer. As it is applied to persons, "to be authentic" means to be genuine, to be true to oneself, not to misrepresent oneself or present
oneself falsely. This common existentiell sense of authenticity sup-
poses that one is able to recognize oneself as a self, independent of
other selves and distinct from the world. In order to be authentic,
genuine, or "truly oneself," one must first be cognizant of oneself as
an "I" or ego, certain of one's distinctive individuality. Necessarily
such a concept of authenticity must derive from or presuppose the

modern discovery of the self-certitude of an independently existing
ego cogito.

Such an existentiell concept of authenticity, however, is not what
I have in mind in the present analysis. In this respect, it is interesting
to note that Heidegger himself never uses the common German terms
authentisch and *Echtheit,* which were available to him in the language
of the day.[59] In fact, he is adamant that existential authenticity (Eigentlichkeit) is not an event that isolates Dasein in the above (onti-
cal) sense of separating it off from the world as an independently
existing "I" or ego. Granted, says Heidegger,

> anxiety individualizes Dasein and thus discloses it as '*solus ipse*'. But
> this existential 'solipsism' is so far from the displacement of putting
> an isolated subject-Thing into the innocuous emptiness of a world-
> less occuring, that in an extreme sense what it does is precisely to
> bring Dasein face to face with its world as world, and thus bring it
> face to face with itself as Being-in-the-world.[60]

The achievement of existential authenticity is thus not the creation of a Self as an independent "I" but rather a disclosure of the primordial uncanniness of one's *own* (*eigen*) finite, factical ground—the
unheimlich, or mysterious, power of one's being thrown into the world
as such. "Resoluteness," writes Heidegger, "as authentic *Being-one's-
Self,* does not detach Dasein from its world, nor does it isolate it so
that it becomes a free-floating 'I'."[61] To the contrary, the authentic
(eigentlich) Self is none other than the "self-possessedness" of Dasein as uncanny, finite possibility.[62] We may assume, then, that Heidegger chose the term *Eigentlichkeit* in order to suggest this
"existential" or ontological sense of authenticity, one that should not
be confused with the usual ontic sense, which carries with it con-
notations of moral worth or approbation. Heidegger writes in his
"Letter on Humanism:" "The terms 'authenticity' and 'un-authentic-

---

[59]No technical reference to either of these terms is to be found in Hildegard Feick, *Index zu Heideggers, "Sein und Zeit"* (Tubingen: Max Niemeyer,
1968).

[60]Heidegger, *Being and Time,* 233.

[61]Ibid., 344.

[62]See Heidegger, *Being and Time,* 233.

ity' [Eigentlichkeit und Uneigentlichkeit] do not signify a moral-ex-
istential or an 'anthropological' distinction, but the 'ecstatic' relation
of man's essence to the truth of Being."[63]

Eigentlichkeit, then, designates this ontological sense of authenticity. It may be translated alternatively by "peculiarity," "owned-
ness," or "self-possessedness." It designates that condition whereby
Dasein becomes what it "properly" is, that is, whereby it comes back
to what is "peculiarly" its own qua Dasein. As Heidegger noted time
and again, however, Dasein is unique not because it exists independently as an isolated ego cogito but rather because it exists ecstati-
cally as a thrown-project. Again from the "Letter on Humanism" we
read: "Existence is here not the actuality of the *ego cogito.* Nor is it
the actuality of subjects that act with and for ech other and in this
way come into their own. . . . Man is rather in his essence ex-sistent
in the openness to Being."[64] *Eigentlichkeit,* then, as returning to oneself, would mean returning to the ground or foundation of one's being-
in-the-world as finite possibility.

Now, I would argue that this conception of authenticity does not
conflict with the notion of anonymity intended in the above description of mythic Dasein as "authentic anonymity." Initially, I note that
Heidegger himself never uses the term anonymity.[65] Granted, he does
speak of Uneigentlichkeit, inauthenticity or "not-being-one's-own."
In this context he refers to *das Man* as an *existentiale* determination
of Dasein's positive constitution. As an ontological characterization
of Dasein, however, *das Man* does not represent a formal concept of
anonymity, sociological, moral, or otherwise. Again, as Heidegger
writes in his "Letter on Humanisms." "What has been said in *Sein und
Zeit* . . . about the word "*man*" (the impersonal one) is not simply
meant to furnish, in passing, a contribution to sociology. In the same
way the word *man* does not simply mean the counterpart—in an eth-
ical existential way—to a person's self-Being."[66] Rather, *das Man* is
the way of designating the Being of inauthentic existence. Yet, within

---

[63]Martin Heidegger, "Letter," 219.

[64]Ibid., 227, 233.

[65]See Feick, *Index.*

[66]Heidegger, "Letter," 208.

this mode of being of das Man we may begin to recognize a possible ontic sense of anonymity. As inauthentic, Dasein is determined existentially by the phenomenon of "falling." Having already turned its back on itself (that is, its being-there as finite possibility), Dasein falls into the tranquillity of the "public domain." Tranquillized, Dasein becomes lost in the superficiality, curiosity, and idle chatter of everyman. "Publicness" (*die Offentlichkeit*) thus denotes a possible ontic sense of anonymity implicit in Heidegger's discussion of the inauthenticity of das Man.[67]

This is not, however, the sense of anonymity to which I refer in developing the present concept of "authentic anonymity." In this respect my own thesis departs radically from Heidegger's analyses in *Being and Time.* The concept of "authentic anonymity" as used in the present context is meant to designate a primordial structure (or existentiale) of Dasein. Accordingly, "anonymity" here has an ontological and not an ontic or sociological significance. Ontically (as we saw above), with anonymity the "I" is fleeing in the face of itself, into the numbing tranquillity of "everyman" (the public domain).

Ontologically, anonymity is of a wholly different order. For the sake of our present discussion, ontological anonymity describes an original, prereflective mode of being, on the far side of the distinction that generates the twin concepts of Self ("I") and group ("everyman"). This ontological sense of anonymity is more clearly articulated in Merleau-Ponty's discussion of fungierende Intentionalität, the prepersonal intentionality of the body-subject—what he calls "l'On."[68] With the concept of "authentic anonymity," I am therefore suggesting that in the prepersonal subjectivity (ontological anonymity) of the body we discover the *unique* (ontologically authentic) self/ground of mythic Dasein as finite possibility represented in the figure of the mythic hero. Mythic authenticity, then, is a return not to the personal self as subject but to the anonymous or prepersonal foundation of being-in-the-world as corporeal *power.*

For Heidegger, then, Dasein exists authentically only through its ability to live toward its end, identifying itself with nothing other than

---

[67]See Heidegger, *Being and Time,* 165, 210, 301, 317, 345.
[68]See Merleau-Ponty, *Phenomenology of Perception,* 240.

its Self in anxious anticipation of the advent of death. Mythic Dasein, on the other hand, returns to itself in the enabling event of being called back to its beginning, authentically being-in-the-world-by-being-the-hero. Now, this mode of being is called "anonymous" because mythic Dasein does not itself possess a name. Yet in identifying with the heroic ancestor it takes the name of that hero. Mythic existence is thus "anonymously" authentic because it is a mode of being-one's-own-through-being-the-Other and only because the Other is the sacred ancestor, a mythic embodiment of the prepersonal power of Dasein's having-to-be.

Mythic anonymity or being lost in ritual identification with a heroic ancestor in illo tempore, ab origine, is precisely that movement of return whereby Dasein is empowered to pull itself back from a mundane present to its sacred past, face the mystery of its finite origin, and authentically temporalize itself as having to be. Accordingly, the narrative-temporal movement of return, whereby mythic Dasein identifies itself with the hero, is an act not of forgetting oneself but of coming back to and finding oneself. Mythic anonymity or identification with the hero is therefore an authentic mode of being in the world, courageously being-toward-the-future in the very event of recollecting, retrieving, and repeating its sacred origin or ontological foundation—that power embodied in the archetypal figure of the mythic hero.

Even Heidegger, however, was not unaware of this inner connection between anonymity and authenticity. He recognizes, for example, that the call of conscience comes from a "who" that is ontically "nothing" whatsoever, that is, nothing with which Dasein is personally familiar. Says Heidegger, "In its 'who' the caller is definable in a 'worldly' way by *nothing* at all,"[69] The caller is as mysterious as the call. Indeed, "it calls [Es ruft] against our expectations and even against our will."[70] As the editors of the English translation of *Being and Time* observe, "the pronoun 'es' [in *Es ruft*] is used quite impersonally [here], and does not refer back to 'the call' itself ('Der Ruf')."[71]

---

[69]Heidegger, *Being and Time,* 321.

[70]Ibid., 320.

[71]Ibid., n. 1.

For this reason I believe Merleau-Ponty's discussion of the prepersonal subjectivity of the body (fungierende Intentionalität) is much
more illuminating of this otherwise ambiguous and obscure mode of
being—*authentic anonymity*—a mode of being that Heidegger was
unable to exhibit fully in terms of his own presuppositions.

Using Merleau-Ponty's language at this point, I would contend that
the call originates in "something anonymous," that prepersonal subjectivity or pouvoir of the lived body-world.[72] It is a call that is of the
self and yet not of the self. Dasein is called from its dispersion in the
public domain (existentiell anonymity), back to l'On, that (ontological) prepersonal anonymity of one's factical thrownness into the
world, the true self or subject of the body.[73] As Heidegger writes, "The
call comes *from* me and yet *from beyond me and over me.*"[74] For this
reason, power and the call find embodiment in the figure of a deity
or sacred ancestor. As Heidegger himself suggests: "If the interpretation continues in this direction, one supplies a possessor for the
power thus posited, or one takes the power itself as a person who
makes himself known—namely God . . . [the divine ancestor or sacred hero]."[75] While Heidegger believes that this is a misinterpreta-
tion of the call as a phenomenon of Dasein, such an intepretation
clearly indicates how the myth maker experiences the hero, the powerful demand of the sacred, as within him yet beyond him. He *is* the
hero, and yet the power of the sacred makes a demand upon him as
if it were other than himself.

Indeed, Heidegger himself goes so far as to suggest that this voice
is "an alien power by which Dasein is dominated."[76] Such is the experience of mythic Dasein, which feels dominated by the power of its
sacred ground. This domination, however, is not to be confused with
being lost in the "public domain." Rather, it is diametrically opposed

---

[72]Merleau-Ponty, *Phenomenology of Perception,* 238.

[73]See Merleau-Ponty, *Phenomenology of Perception,* 240; Kwant, *Phenomenological Philosophy,* and Alphonso Lingis, "Sense and Non-sense in
the Sexed Body," *Cultural Hermeneutics* 4 (1877): 345-65.

[74]Heidegger, *Being and Time,* 320.

[75]Ibid.

[76]Ibid.

to the world of das Man. This alien power is Dasein itself in its own uncanny thrownness, its prepersonal and powerful ground. "The caller is ... primordial, thrown Being-in-the-world as the "not-at-home"—the bare 'that-it-is' in the "nothing" of the world. The caller is unfamiliar to the everyday they-self; it is something like an *alien* voice."[77] What could be more alien to das Man, however, than the nothingness of the world that is revealed in the anxiety of Dasein's coming face to face with its own thrownness, wherein its very potentiality (power) for being-in-the-world is at stake?[78] Thus, as Heidegger concludes, this "call whose mood has been attuned by anxiety makes it possible first and foremost for Dasein to project itself upon its ownmost *potentiality-for-Being.*"[79]

In brief, I have argued that mythic Dasein, with its unique capacity to collect itself from the mundanity of "worldly" affairs through identification with the mythic hero of the group, is called back to its own prepersonal (ambiguous, anonymous) foundation, namely, its finite factical ground. I contend that such a being must be understood as demonstrating a fundamental mode of authentic existence, anxiously facing its own potentiality for being at all in the resolute recollection of its awe-inspiring, powerful, and sacred ground.

---

[77]Ibid., 321.

[78]Ibid., 321-22.

[79]Ibid., 322.

Sein zur Entstehung:
A Conclusion

The meaning of myth is a recurrent theme in anthropology and in the history and philosophy of religion, as well as in biblical and philosophical theology. Traditionally this problem was addressed as a linguistic issue, under the assumption that myth-analysis represented a special case for philology or literary hermeneutics. More recently the question of myth has been addressed as an epistemological concern. From Ernst Cassirer to Claude Lévi-Strauss, myth-analysis has been considered increasingly in terms of a philosophical or structural analysis of consciousness and the problem of knowledge. With other contemporary thinkers, such as George Gusdorf and Paul Ricoeur, we have begun to witness yet another mode of access to myth-analysis, the examination of myth primarily as a concern of philosophical anthropology.

In this book, I have viewed myth ontologically in light of this philosophical-anthropological problematic. My guiding assumption has been that myth may be understood as a particular mode of being-in-the-world. In order to display the meaning of mythic existence, I took as my point of departure the descriptions offered by existential phenomenology. In particular, I found that the combined analyses of Martin Heidegger and Maurice Merleau-Ponty offered a unique perspective from which to disclose the *structure* of mythic existence in terms of the prepersonal subjectivity of the body and the *meaning* of this (mythic) subjectivity in view of the constitutive horizon of temporality.

In *Being and Time,* Heidegger demonstrated that authenticity—returning to one's ownmost possibility—may be realized in the event of *Sein zum Tode.* In being-toward-death, Dasein recalls the possibility of its own impossibility, that is, the possibility of its coming to an end. In that moment of anxiously anticipating death, existence is rescued from arbitrary dispersion in the public domain and returns to itself (its *Grund*) as a finite possibility.

On the other hand, I have demonstrated that, in the retrieval of an archetypal past, where mythic Dasein recovers those heroic deeds ab origine, we witness a similar event of authenticity—coming back to one's ownmost possibility—in the event of *Sein-zur-Entstehung.* Overdetermined by the phenomenon of "being-in-the-throw" or "having to be," mythic Dasein finds itself *already* given over to the world, enveloped within an aura of prepersonal power. This power finds embodiment in the figures of sacred heroes. Retrieving those heroic deeds and identifying oneself with the sacred ancestors, mythic Dasein comes back to its factical ground. Existence thus comes face to face with the power of its being-in-the-world in the awe-filled realization of its own finite foundation. Being-toward-the-beginning, mythic Dasein resolutely faces its ownmost possibility (now from the other side), the possibility of its never having been at all.

Thus while Heidegger correctly recognized Eigentlichkeit in the resolute anticipation of one's coming-to-an-end, we must not fail to recognize an authentic mode of being displayed in the resolute recollection of one's coming-to-be. In other words, the possibility of one's own impossibility, namely, one's ownmost potentiality for being, can be read backward as well as forward. Dasein may authentically "gather up" (recall or retrieve) its very (eigen) foundation either by anticipating the telos or recollecting the *arche* of finite existence within the world.

Still, if "end" and "beginning" are always outstanding moments for each individual Dasein, then just as man can never experience *being at* his own end, so too he can never experience *being at* his own beginning. In either case—anticipatory or recollective—what Dasein actually achieves is a recovery of its primordial foundation as finite possibility. Authenticity indicates the *fact* of that retrieval, while anticipation (*Sein zum Tode*) and recollection (*Sein zur Entstehung*) indicate the *how* of that event. In either case, an outstanding limit of finite existence is realized, and Dasein is rescued from the self-forgetfulness of its worldly (profane) involvements, thrust back upon its own powerful/sacred ground.

We have noticed, finally, one significant difference between these two modes of authenticity. Authentic being-toward-death is an event that recalls Dasein back to itself (its ground) by calling it out of the group, away from the "anonymous" domination of das Man. Authentic being-toward-the-beginning, on the other hand, is an event that calls the myth maker back to his ground by calling him mythically into the group, identifying him with the sacred hero—the mythic embodiment of power—the *anonymous* power of his own finite foundation.

Selected Bibliography

Akinnaso, F. Niyi. "The Consequences of Literacy in Pragmatic and Theoretical Perspectives." *Anthropology and Education Quarterly* 12:3 (1981): 163-200.

Arendt, Hannah. *The Life of the Mind.* New York: Harcourt Brace Jovanovich, 1981.

Barden, Garrett. "The Intention of Truth in Mythic Consciousness." In P. McShane, ed., *Language, Truth, and Meaning.* South Bend IN: University of Notre Dame Press, 1972.

_____. "Reflections of Time." *Human Context* 5 (Summer 1973): 331-43.

Barndt, C. "The Concept of the Primitive." In A. Montagu, ed., *The Concept of the Primitive.* New York: Collier-Macmillan, 1976.

Basso, Keith. Review of *The Domestication of the Savage Mind,* by Jack Goody. *Language and Society* 9:2 (1980): 72-80.

Benveniste, Emile. *Some Problems in General Linguistics.* Leiden: Brill, 1971.

Berger, P., and Luckmann, T. *The Social Construction of Reality.* New York: Doubleday, 1967.

Bidney, David. "Myth, Symbolism, and Truth." In T. Sebeok, ed., *Myth: A Symposium.* Philadelphia: American Folklore Society, 1955.

Breckon, Gary. "Cassirer's Genealogy of the 'I'." *Idealistic Studies* 1 (Summer 1971): 278-91.

Bultmann, Rudolph. "The New Testament and Mythology." In H. W. Bartsch, ed., *Kerygma and Myth.* New York: Harper and Row, 1961.

Carothers, J. C. "Culture, Psychiatry, and the Written Word." *Psychiatry* 22 (1959): 307-20.

_____. "Hysteria, Psychopathy, and the Magic Word." *Psychiatry* 21 (1958): 93-103.

Carpenter, Richard. " 'Ontological Naivete' and the Truth of Myth." *Personalist* 44 (1963): 337-53.

Cassirer, Ernst. *The Myth of the State.* New Haven: Yale University Press, 1950.

_____. *The Philosophy of Symbolic Forms.* Trans. C. R. Manheim. New Haven: Yale University Press, 1972.

Charbonnier, Georges. " 'Primitive' and 'Civilized' Peoples: A Conversation with Claude Lévi-Strauss." In R. Disch, *The Future of Literacy.* Englewood Cliffs: Prentice-Hall, 1973.

Cohen, Percy. "Theories of Myth." *Man,* n.s. 4 (1969): 337-53.

Conn, Walter. "Primitive Consciousness—Mythic, Symbolic, Prelogical: A Cognitive Analysis." *American Catholic Philosophical Association, Proceedings* 45 (1971): 147-157.

Coyne, Margaret Urban. "Merleau-Ponty on Language." *International Philosophical Quarterly* 20 (Spring 1980): 307-26.

Cross, F. M. *Canaanite Myth and Hebrew Epic.* Cambridge MA: Harvard University Press, 1973.

Dagenais, James. "The Scientific Study of Myth and Ritual: A Lost Cause." *Human Context* 6 (1974): 586-620.

D'Arcy, Martin. *No Absent God.* London: Routledge and Kegan Paul, 1962.

Dardel, Eric. "The Mythic." *Diogenes* 7 (Summer 1954): 33-51.

Derrida, Jacques. "The Violence of the Letter: From Lévi-Strauss to Rousseau." In *Of Grammatology.* Baltimore: Johns Hopkins University Press, 1976.

Descombes, Vincent. *Modern French Philosophy.* Trans. L. Scott-Fox and J. M. Harding. London: Cambridge University Press, 1980.

Dilthey, Wilhelm. *Pattern and Meaning in History.* Ed. H. P. Rickman. New York: Harper and Row, 1962.

Eliade, Mircea. *Cosmos and History.* Trans. W. Trask. New York: Harper and Row, 1959.

_____. "Methodological Remarks on the Study of Religious Symbolism." In *History of Religions: Essays in Methodology.* Chicago: University of Chicago Press, 1973.

_____. *Myth and Reality.* Trans. W. Trask. New York: Harper and Row, 1962.

_____. *Patterns in Comparative Religion.* Trans. R. Sheed. New York: Meridian, 1963.

_____. *The Sacred and the Profane.* New York: Harper and Row, 1962.

_____. *Shamanism.* Bollingen Series. Princeton: Princeton University Press, 1972.

Elkin, A. P. *The Australian Aborigines.* London, 1938.

Evans-Pritchard. E. E. *The Nuer.* Oxford: Clarendon Press, 1940.

Feick, Hildegard. *Index zu Heideggers "Sein und Zeit."* Tubingen: Max Niemeyer, 1968.

Finnegan, Ruth. "Literacy versus Non-literacy: The Great Divide?" In R. Finnegan and R. Horton, *Modes of Thought.* London: Ralser and Ralser, 1973.

Firth, Raymond. *Tikopia Ritual and Belief.* Boston: Beacon, 1968.

Frankfort, Henri et al. *Before Philosophy.* Baltimore: Penguin, 1972.

_____. *The Birth of Civilization in the Ancient Near East.* New York: Doubleday, 1956.

Frazer, James George. *The Belief in Immortality.* London: Cambridge University Press, 1913.

Gadamer, Hans-Georg. *Philosophical Hermeneutics.* Trans. D. Linge. Berkeley: University of California Press, 1977.

_____. *Truth and Method.* New York: Seabury, 1975.

Gale, I. F. "Aboriginal Time." *Folklore* 91:1 (1980): 3-10.

Gaster, Theodore. *Thespis: Ritual, Myth, and Drama in the Ancient Near East.* New York: Norton, 1977.

Geertz, Clifford. *The Interpretation of Cultures.* New York: Basic Books, 1973.

Gill, Sam. *Beyond "The Primitive": The Religions of Nonliterate Peoples.* Englewood Cliffs: Prentice-Hall, 1982.

Gillan, Garth, ed. *The Horizons of the Flesh.* Carbondale: Southern Illinois University Press, 1973.

Goody, Jack. *The Domestication of the Savage Mind.* New York: Cambridge University Press, 1978.

_____. "Religion and Ritual: A Definitional Problem." *British Journal of Sociology* 12 (1961): 142-64.

Goody, Jack, and Watt, Ian. "The Consequences of Literacy." *Comparative Studies in Society and History* 15 (1962-1963): 304-45.

_____ "Literate Culture: Some General Considerations." In R. Disch, ed., *The Future of Literacy.* Englewood Cliffs: Prentice-Hall, 1973.

Gough, Kathleen. "Implications of Literacy in Traditional China and India." In J. Goody, *Literacy in Traditional Societies.* Cambridge: Cambridge University Press, 1968.

Greenfield. Patricia. "Oral or Written Language: The Consequences of Cognitive Development in Africa, the United States, and England." *Language and Speech* 15 (1972): 169-78.

Guerriere, Daniel. "The Structure of Mythic Existence." *Personalist* 55 (1974): 261-72.

Gurwitsch, Aron. "Problems of the Life-World." In M. Natanson, ed., *Phenomenology and Social Reality: Essays in Memory of Alfred Schutz.* The Hague: Martinus Nijhoff, 1962.

Gusdorf, Georges. *Mythe et Métaphysique.* Paris: Flammarion, 1953.

_____. *Speaking.* Trans. P. Brockelman. Evanston: Northwestern University Press, 1965.

Hall, Ronald. "The Origin of Alienation: Some Kierkegaardian Reflections on Merleau-Ponty's Phenomenology of the Body." *International Journal for the Philosophy of Religion* 12 (1981): 111-22.

Hallowell, A. "Temporal Orientation in Western Civilization and in a Preliterate Society." *American Anthropologist* 39 (1937): 647-70.

Hart, James. "Mythic World as World." *International Philosophical Quarterly* 15 (1975): 51-69.

_____. "Towards a Phenomenology of Nostalgia." *Man and World* 6 (November 1973): 397-420.

Heidegger, Martin. *Being and Time.* Trans. Macquarrie and J. E. Robinson. New York: Harper and Row, 1962.

_____. *An Introduction to Metaphysics.* Trans. R. Manheim. New Haven: Yale University Press, 1975.

_____. "Letter on Humanism." In N. Languilli, ed., *The Existentialist Tradition.* Garden City: Doubleday, 1971.

_____. *The Piety of Thinking.* Ed. J. Hart and J. Maraldo. Bloomington: Indiana University Press, 1976.

_____. "Review of Ernst Cassirer's *Mythical Thought.*" In J. G. Hart and J. C. Maraldo, eds., *The Piety of Thinking.* Bloomington: Indiana University Press, 1976.

_____. *Sein und Zeit.* Tubingen: Max Niemeyer, 1979.

_____. *Vorträge und Aufsätze.* Pfullingen: G. Neske, 1954.

Heidel, Alexander. *The Babylonian Genesis.* Chicago: University of Chicago Press, 1972.

Herskovits, M. J. *Cultural Anthropology.* New York: Knopf, 1955.

_____. *Man and His Works: The Science of Cultural Anthropology.* New York: Knopf, 1948.

Hofstadter, Albert. *Truth and Art.* New York: Columbia University Press, 1965.

Horton, Robin. "African Traditional Thought and Modern Science." In B. Wilson, ed., *Rationality.* Oxford: Blackwell, 1970.

Husserl, Edmund. *Cartesian Meditations.* Trans. Dorian Cairns. The Hague: Martinus Nijhoff, 1967.

_____. *The Crisis of the European Sciences and Transcendental Phenomenology.* Trans. D. Carr. Evanston: Northwestern University Press, 1970.

_____. *The Idea of Phenomenology.* Trans. William P. Alston and G. Nakhnikian. The Hague: Martinus Nijhoff, 1968.

_____. *The Paris Lectures.* Trans. Peter Koestenbaum. The Hague: Martinus Nijhoff, 1970.

_____. " 'Phenomenology': Edmund Husserl's Article for the *Encyclopaedia Britannica* (1927)." Trans. R. E. Palmer. In R. Zaner and D. Ihde, eds., *Phenomenology and Existentialism.* New York: Capricorn, 1973.

"Husserl's Inaugural Lecture at Freiburg im Breisgau (1917)." In L. E. Embree, ed., *Life-World and Consciousness: Essays for Aron Gurwitsch.* Evanston: Northwestern University Press, 1972.

Ihde, Don. "Rationality and Myth." *Journal of Thought* 2 (1967): 10-18.

Jacobsen, Thorkild. *Treasures of Darkness.* New Haven: Yale University Press, 1978.

Johnson, Roger. *The Origins of Demythologizing.* Leiden: Brill, 1974.

Jonas, Hans. *The Phenomenon of Life.* New York: Delta, 1968.

Kaelin, Eugene. *Art and Existence.* Lewisburg: Bucknell, 1970.

Keesing, Felix. *Cultural Anthropology.* New York: Holt, Rinehart and Winston, 1958.

Kelber, Werner. *The Oral and the Written Gospel.* Philadelphia: Fortress, 1983.

Kierkegaard, Søren. *Repetition.* New York: Harper and Row, 1964.

Kockelmanns, Joseph. *Martin Heidegger: A First Introduction to His Philosophy.* Pittsburgh: Duquesne University Press, 1965.

_____, ed. *On Heidegger and Language.* Evanston: Northwestern University Press, 1972.

_____. "On Myth and Its Relationship to Hermeneutics." *Cultural Hermeneutics* 1 (1973): 47-85.

Kohler, Wolfgang. *The Selected Papers.* Ed. Mary Henle. New York: Liveright, 1971.

Krader, Lawrence. "Primary Reification and Primitive Mythology." *Transactions of the New York Academy of Sciences* 30 (1968): 51-73.

Krolick, Sanford. "Gesture and Myth: A Phenomenological Reflection on Myth and Traditional Culture." *Man and World* 14:2 (1981): 201-11.

Kwant, Remy. *The Phenomenological Philosophy of Merleau-Ponty.* Pittsburgh: Duquesne University Press, 1963.

_____. *Phenomenology of Expression.* New Jersey: Humanities Press, 1969.

_____. "We Inhabit the World." *Humanitas* 12 (November 1976): 299-309.

Landgrebe, Ludwig. *Major Problems in Contemporary European Philosophy.* Trans. Kurt F. Reinhardt. New York: Frederick Ungar, 1966.

Langan, Thomas. *The Meaning of Heidegger.* New York: Columbia University Press, 1971.

_____. *Merleau-Ponty's Critique of Reason.* New Haven: Yale University Press, 1966.

Leach, Edmund. *Rethinking Anthropology.* London: Athlone, 1961.

_____. "Sermons from a Man on a Ladder." A review of *Mephistopheles and the Androgyne,* by Mircea Eliade. *New York Review of Books,* 20 October 1966, pp. 26-29.

Lee, Dorothy. "Codification of Reality: Lineal and Nonlineal." In *Freedom and Culture.* Englewood Cliffs: Prentice-Hall, 1959.

Leenhardt, Maurice. *Do Kamo.* Trans. B. Miller Gulati. Chicago: University of Chicago Press, 1979.

Lévi-Strauss, Claude. "Introduction: History and Anthropology." In *Structural Anthropology.* Garden City: Doubleday, 1967.

_____. *Myth and Meaning.* New York: Shocken, 1979.

_____. *Mythologiques.* Vol. 1 in *The Raw and the Cooked.* New York: Harper and Row, 1979.

_____. *The Savage Mind.* Chicago, 1966.

Levy, Marion Joseph. *The Structure of Society.* Princeton: Princeton University Press, 1952.

Levy-Bruhl, Lucien. *The Notebooks on Primitive Mentality.* Trans. P. Riviere. New York: Harper and Row, 1978.

Lingis, Alphonso. "Intentionality and Corporeity." In Ann-Teresa Tymieniecka, ed., *Analecta Husserliana,* vol. 1. Dordrecht: Reidel, 1971.

_____. "Sense and Non-sense in the Sexed Body." *Cultural Hermeneutics* 4 (1977): 345-65.

Linton, Ralph, ed. *The Tree of Culture.* New York: Knopf, 1955.

Maddock, Kenneth. *The Australian Aborigines.* London: Allen Lane, 1973.

Mead, Margaret, and Calas, Nicholas. *Primitive Heritage.* New York: Random House, 1953.

Mehta, J. L. *Martin Heidegger: The Way and the Vision.* Honolulu: University of Hawaii Press, 1976.

Mendelsohn, Isaac, ed. *Religion of the Ancient Near East.* New York: Liberal Arts Press, 1955.

Merleau-Ponty, Maurice. *Consciousness and the Acquisition of Language.* Trans. Hugh Silverman. Evanston: Northwestern University Press, 1973.

_____. *Phénoménologie de la perception.* Paris: Gallimard, 1945.

_____. *Phenomenology of Perception.* Trans. Colin Smith. Garden City NJ: Humanities Press, 1962.

_____. *Signs.* Trans. R. C. McCleary. Evanston: Northwestern University Press, 1964.

Muck, Otto. *The Transcendental Method.* New York: Herder and Herder, 1968.

Natanson, Maurice. "Phenomenology, Anonymity, and Alienation." *New Literary History* 10 (1979): 533-46.

_____. "The Problem of Anonymity in Gurwitsch and Schutz." *Research in Phenomenology* 5 (1975): 51-56.

Olson, David R. "From Utterance to Text: The Bias of Language in Speech and Writing." *Harvard Education Review* 47 (1977): 257-81.

O'Neill, John. *Perception, Expression, and History.* Evanston: Northwestern University Press, 1970.

Ong, Walter. *The Presence of the Word.* Minneapolis: University of Minnesota Press, 1981.

_____. "Space and Intellect in Renaissance Symbolism." *Explorations* 4 (1955): 95-100.

Palmer, R. E. *Hermeneutics.* Evanston: Northwestern University Press, 1969.

Parratt, John. "Time in Traditional African Thought." *Religion* 7 (Autumn 1977): 117-126.

Penner, Hans. "Is Phenomenology a Method for the Study of Religion?" *Bucknell Review* 18:3 (Winter 1970): 29-54.

Pierce, David. "Lévi-Strauss: The Problematic Self and Myth." *International Philosophical Quarterly* 19 (1979): 381-406.

Plato. "The Phaedrus." In E. Hamilton and H. Cairns, *The Collected Dialogues.* Bollingen Series. Princeton: Princeton University Press, 1973.

Radcliffe-Brown, A. R. *Structure and Function in Primitive Society.* London: Cohen and West, 1952.

Ray, Benjamin. "Death, Kingship, and Royal Ancestors in Buganda." In F. Reynolds and E. Waugh, eds., *Religious Encounters with Death.* University Park: Pennsylvania State University Press, 1977.

Richardson, A. *A Theological Word Book of the Bible.* New York: Macmillan, 1977.

Ricoeur, Paul. *Fallible Man.* Trans. C. Kelbley. Chicago: Regnery, 1965.

_____. "The Hermeneutical Function of Distanciation." *Philosophy Today* 17 (1973): 129-41.

_____. "The Human Experience of Time and Narrative." *Research in Phenomenology* 9 (1979): 17-34.

_____. *Interpretation Theory.* Fort Worth: T.C.U. Texas Christian University Press, 1976.

_____. *The Symbolism of Evil.* Boston: Beacon, 1969.

Rieff, Philip. "Origins of Freud's Political Psychology." *Journal of the History of Ideas* 17 (April 1956): 235-49.

Ryle, Gilbert. "Heidegger's *Sein und Zeit.* " In M. Murray, ed., *Heidegger and Modern Philosophy.* New Haven: Yale University Press, 1978.

Sadler, A. W. "Myth as Collapsed History." *Horizon* 3 (June 1976): 221-42.

Schneidau, H. *Sacred Discontent.* Baton Rouge: Louisiana State University Press, 1976.

Schrag, Calvin. "Heidegger on Repetition and Historical Understanding." *Philosophy East and West* 20 (1970): 287-95.

_____. *Radical Reflection and the Origin of the Human Sciences.* Bloomington: Indiana University Press, 1980.

Schutz, Alfred. *Collected Papers.* Ed. M. Natanson. The Hague: Martinus Nijhoff, 1962.

Shalvey, Thomas. "Lévi-Strauss and Mythology." *American Catholic Philosophical Association, Proceedings.* 45 (1971): 114-19.

Sheehan, Thomas. "Getting to the Topic: The New Edition of *Wegmarken.*" *Research in Phenomenology* 7 (1977): 299-316.

Shiner, Larry. "Sacred Space, Profane Space." *Journal of the American Academy of Religion* 40:4 (December 1972): 425-36.

Smart, Ninian. "Cross-Religious Comparisons." In Walter Capps, ed., *Ways of Understanding Religion.* New York: Macmillan, 1972.

Smith, Jonathan A. "Adde Parvum Parvo Magnus Acervus." In *Map Is Not the Territory.* Leiden: Brill, 1978.

_____. "I Am a Parrot (Red)." *History of Religions* 11:4 (May 1972): 391-413.

Spencer, B., and Gillan, F. J. *The Arunta.* London, 1927.

Spiegelberg, Herbert. *The Phenomenological Movement.* The Hague: Martinus Nijhoff, 1978.

Stanner, W. E. H. *White Man Got No Dreaming: Essays, 1938-1973.* Canberra: Australian National University Press, 1979.

Tait, David. *The Konkomba of Northern Ghana.* London: Oxford University Press, 1961.

Taminiaux, Jacques. "Heidegger and Husserl's *Logical Investigations:* In Remembrance of Heidegger's Last Seminar (Zahringen, 1973)." *Research in Phenomenology* 8 (1978): 58-83.

Tillich, Paul. *Systematic Theology.* Chicago, 1973.

Tonkinson, Robert. *The Mardudjara Aborigines: Living the Dream in Australia's Desert.* New York: Holt, Rinehart and Winston, 1978.

Turner, Victor. *Dramas, Fields, and Metaphors.* Ithaca: Cornell University Press, 1974.

Vail. L. M. *Heidegger and Ontological Difference.* University Park: Pennsylvania State University Press, 1972.

Van der Leeuw, Gerhardus. *Religion in Essence and Manifestation.* New York: Harper and Row, 1963.

Van Gennep, A. *Rites of Passage.* Chicago, 1972.

Verene, David. *Symbol, Myth, and Culture.* New Haven: Yale University Press, 1979.

Volkmann-Schluck, K. H. "The Problem of Language." In G. Ballard and Charles Scott, eds., *Martin Heidegger in Europe and America.* The Hague: Martinus Nijhoff, 1973.

von Schoenborn, Alexander. "Heidegger's Articulation of Falling." In J. Sallis, ed., *Philosophy and Archaic Experience.* Pittsburgh: Duquesne University Press, 1982.

Whorf, B. L. *Language, Thought, and Reality.* New York: Wiley, 1959.

Williams, D. C. "Acoustic Space." *Explorations* 4 (1955): 15-20.

Wilson, John. *The Culture of Ancient Egypt.* Chicago: University of Chicago Press, 1965.

Wolf, Robert. "Cassirer and the Philosophic Study of Myth." *American Catholic Philosophical Association, Proceedings* 45 (1971): 104-13.

Young, M., ed. *The Ethnography of Malinowski.* London: Routledge and Kegan Paul, 1979.

Zimmerman, Michael. *Eclipse of the Self.* Athens: Ohio University Press, 1982.

_____. "Heidegger and Bultmann: Egoism, Sinfulness, and Inauthenticity." *Modern Schoolman* 58 (November 1980): 1-20.

_____. "On Discriminating Everydayness, Unownedness, and Falling in *Being and Time.*" *Research in Phenomenology* 5 (1975): 109-27.

Subject Index

Author Index